HMH SCIENCE DIMENSIONS™
WAVES AND THEIR APPLICATIONS

Module L

This Write-In Book belongs to

_____

Teacher/Room

_____

Houghton Mifflin Harcourt™

Consulting Authors

Michael A. DiSpezio

Global Educator
North Falmouth,
Massachusetts

Michael DiSpezio has authored many HMH instructional programs for Science and Mathematics. He has also authored numerous trade books and multimedia programs on various topics and hosted dozens of studio and location broadcasts for various organizations in the U.S. and worldwide. Most recently, he has been working with educators to provide strategies for implementing the Next Generation Science Standards, particularly the science and engineering practices, cross-cutting concepts, and the use of Evidence Notebooks. To all his projects, he brings his extensive background in science, his expertise in classroom teaching at the elementary, middle, and high school levels, and his deep experience in producing interactive and engaging instructional materials.

Marjorie Frank

Science Writer and Content-Area Reading Specialist
Brooklyn, New York

An educator and linguist by training, a writer and poet by nature, Marjorie Frank has authored and designed a generation of instructional materials in all subject areas, including past HMH Science programs. Her other credits include authoring science issues of an award-winning children's magazine, writing game-based digital assessments, developing blended learning materials for young children, and serving as instructional designer and co-author of pioneering school-to-work software. In addition, she has served on the adjunct faculty of Hunter, Manhattan, and Brooklyn Colleges, teaching courses in science methods, literacy, and writing. For *HMH Science Dimensions™*, she has guided the development of our K–2 strands and our approach to making connections between NGSS and Common Core ELA/literacy standards.

Acknowledgments

Cover credits: (speakers) ©Houghton Mifflin Harcourt; (ear buds) restyler/Shutterstock.

Section Header Master Art: (waves, computer artwork) ©Alfred Pasieka/Science Source

Printed in the U.S.A.

ISBN   978-0-544-86105-3

4 5 6 7 8 9 10 0877   25 24 23 22 21 20 19 18 17

4500645473   A B C D E F G

Michael R. Heithaus, Ph.D.

Dean, College Of Arts, Sciences & Education Professor, Department Of Biological Sciences
Florida International University
Miami, Florida

Mike Heithaus joined the FIU Biology Department in 2003, has served as Director of the Marine Sciences Program and Executive Director of the School of Environment, Arts, and Society, which brings together the natural and social sciences and humanities to develop solutions to today's environmental challenges. He now serves as Dean of the College of Arts, Sciences & Education. His research focuses on predator-prey interactions and the ecological importance of large marine species. He has helped to guide the development of Life Science content in *HMH Science Dimensions™*, with a focus on strategies for teaching challenging content as well as the science and engineering practices of analyzing data and using computational thinking.

Cary I. Sneider, Ph.D.

Associate Research Professor
Portland State University
Portland, Oregon

While studying astrophysics at Harvard, Cary Sneider volunteered to teach in an Upward Bound program and discovered his real calling as a science teacher. After teaching middle and high school science in Maine, California, Costa Rica and Micronesia, he settled for nearly three decades at Lawrence Hall of Science in Berkeley, California, where he developed skills in curriculum development and teacher education. Over his career Cary directed more than 20 federal, state, and foundation grant projects, and was a writing team leader for the Next Generation Science Standards. He has been instrumental in ensuring *HMH Science Dimensions™* meets the high expectations of the NGSS and provides an effective three-dimensional learning experience for all students.

Program Advisors

Paul D. Asimow
Eleanor and John R. McMillan Professor of Geology and Geochemistry
California Institute of Technology
Pasadena, California

Dr. Eileen Cashman
Professor
Humboldt State University
Arcata, California

Elizabeth A. De Stasio
Raymond J. Herzog Professor of Science
Lawrence University
Appleton, Wisconsin

Perry Donham
Lecturer
Boston University
Boston, Massachusetts

Shila Garg, Ph.D.
Emerita Professor of Physics Former Dean of Faculty & Provost
The College of Wooster
Wooster, Ohio

Tatiana A. Krivosheev
Professor of Physics
Clayton State University
Morrow, Georgia

Mark B. Moldwin
Professor of Space Sciences and Engineering
University of Michigan
Ann Arbor, Michigan

Kelly Y. Neiles, Ph.D.
Assistant Professor of Chemistry
St. Mary's College of Maryland
St. Mary's City, Maryland

Dr. Sten Odenwald
Astronomer
NASA Goddard Spaceflight Center
Greenbelt, Maryland

Bruce W. Schafer
Executive Director
Oregon Robotics Tournament & Outreach Program
Beaverton, Oregon

Barry A. Van Deman
President and CEO
Museum of Life and Science
Durham, North Carolina

Kim Withers, Ph.D.
Assistant Professor
Texas A&M University-Corpus Christi
Corpus Christi, Texas

Adam D. Woods, Ph.D.
Professor
California State University, Fullerton
Fullerton, California

Classroom Reviewers

You are a scientist!
You are naturally curious.

Have you ever wondered . . .

- why is it difficult to catch a fly?
- how a new island can appear in an ocean?
- how to design a great tree house?
- how a spacecraft can send messages across the solar system?

HMH SCIENCE DIMENSIONS™

will *SPARK* your curiosity!

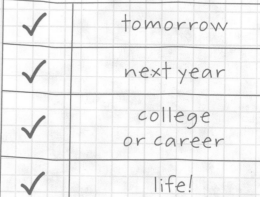

AND prepare you for

✓	tomorrow
✓	next year
✓	college or career
✓	life!

Where do you see yourself in 15 years?

Observe

Collect Data

Be a scientist.
Work like real scientists work.

Analyze

Be an engineer.
Solve problems like engineers do.

Define Problems

Test Solutions

STEM

Gather Information

Think Critically

Explain your world.
Start by asking questions.

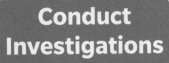**Conduct Investigations**

Wilson/Shutterstock; (b) ©PhotoAlto/Alamy

Collaborate

Develop Explanations

There's more than one way to the answer. What's YOURS?

Construct Arguments

YOUR Program

Write-In Book:

- a brand-new and innovative textbook that will guide you through your next generation curriculum, including your hands-on lab program

Interactive Online Student Edition:

- a complete online version of your textbook enriched with videos, interactivities, animations, simulations, and room to enter data, draw, and store your work

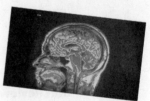

More tools are available online to help you practice and learn science, including:

- Hands-On Labs
- Science and Engineering Practices Handbook
- Crosscutting Concepts Handbook
- English Language Arts Handbook
- Math Handbook

Contents

UNIT 1

Waves

Lesson 1
Introduction to Waves 4
 Hands-On Lab Model Two Types of Waves 10

Hands-On Lab Investigate Waves 14

People in Science James West, Research Scientist 17

Lesson 2
The Behavior of Mechanical Waves 22

Hands-On Lab Generate Mechanical Waves 26

Lesson 3
Light Waves 40

Hands-On Lab Model Specific Wave Properties 52

Lesson 4
The Behavior of Light Waves 60

Hands-On Lab Make a Penny Disappear 67

Hands-On Lab Light Up a Maze 73

Unit Review 81
ENGINEER IT Unit Performance Task 85

On a rainy night in the city, light shines brightly in interesting ways from the buildings, the water, and the camera lens.

UNIT 2

Information Transfer

Lesson 1
Communication and Waves 90

(hand icon) Hands-On Lab Encode a Message 94

Lesson 2
Analog and Digital Signals..106

(hand icon) Hands-On Lab Transmit and Record a Signal..............................116

Lesson 3
Communication Technology 124

(hand icon) Hands-On Lab Explore How Technology Can Improve Scientific Studies.......137

Careers in Engineering Cell Tower Technician.............................139

Unit Review 145
ENGINEER IT Unit Performance Task 149

Devices that use signals are designed for many different situations. Some may need to operate without electrical energy or withstand a range of weather conditions.

Whether you are in the lab or in the field, you are responsible for your own safety and the safety of others. To fulfill these responsibilities and avoid accidents, be aware of the safety of your classmates as well as your own safety at all times. Take your lab work and field work seriously, and behave appropriately. Elements of safety to keep in mind are shown below and on the following pages.

Safety in the Lab

- [ ] Be sure you understand the materials, your procedure, and the safety rules before you start an investigation in the lab.

- [ ] Know where to find and how to use fire extinguishers, eyewash stations, shower stations, and emergency power shut-offs.

- [ ] Use proper safety equipment. Always wear personal protective equipment, such as eye protection and gloves, when setting up labs, during labs, and when cleaning up.

- [ ] Do not begin until your teacher has told you to start. Follow directions.

- [ ] Keep the lab neat and uncluttered. Clean up when you are finished. Report all spills to your teacher immediately. Watch for slip/fall and trip/fall hazards.

- [ ] If you or another student are injured in any way, tell your teacher immediately, even if the injury seems minor.

- [ ] Do not take any food or drink into the lab. Never take any chemicals out of the lab.

Safety in the Field

- [ ] Be sure you understand the goal of your fieldwork and the proper way to carry out the investigation before you begin fieldwork.

- [ ] Use proper safety equipment and personal protective equipment, such as eye protection, that suits the terrain and the weather.

- [ ] Follow directions, including appropriate safety procedures as provided by your teacher.

- [ ] Do not approach or touch wild animals. Do not touch plants unless instructed by your teacher to do so. Leave natural areas as you found them.

- [ ] Stay with your group.

- [ ] Use proper accident procedures, and let your teacher know about a hazard in the environment or an accident immediately, even if the hazard or accident seems minor.

Safety Symbols

To highlight specific types of precautions, the following symbols are used throughout the lab program. Remember that no matter what safety symbols you see within each lab, all safety rules should be followed at all times.

Dress Code

- Wear safety goggles (or safety glasses as appropriate for the activity) at all times in the lab as directed. If chemicals get into your eye, flush your eyes immediately for a minimum of 15 minutes.
- Do not wear contact lenses in the lab.
- Do not look directly at the sun or any intense light source or laser.
- Wear appropriate protective non-latex gloves as directed.
- Wear an apron or lab coat at all times in the lab as directed.
- Tie back long hair, secure loose clothing, and remove loose jewelry. Remove acrylic nails when working with active flames.
- Do not wear open-toed shoes, sandals, or canvas shoes in the lab.

Glassware and Sharp Object Safety

- Do not use chipped or cracked glassware.
- Use heat-resistant glassware for heating or storing hot materials.
- Notify your teacher immediately if a piece of glass breaks.
- Use extreme care when handling any sharp and pointed instruments.
- Do not cut an object while holding the object unsupported in your hands. Place the object on a suitable cutting surface, and always cut in a direction away from your body.

Chemical Safety

- If a chemical gets on your skin, on your clothing, or in your eyes, rinse it immediately for a minimum of 15 minutes (using the shower, faucet, or eyewash station), and alert your teacher.
- Do not clean up spilled chemicals unless your teacher directs you to do so.
- Do not inhale any gas or vapor unless directed to do so by your teacher. If you are instructed to note the odor of a substance, wave the fumes toward your nose with your hand. This is called wafting. Never put your nose close to the source of the odor.
- Handle materials that emit vapors or gases in a well-ventilated area.
- Keep your hands away from your face while you are working on any activity.

Safety Symbols, continued

Electrical Safety

- Do not use equipment with frayed electrical cords or loose plugs.
- Do not use electrical equipment near water or when clothing or hands are wet.
- Hold the plug housing when you plug in or unplug equipment. Do not pull on the cord.
- Use only GFI protected electrical receptacles.

Heating and Fire Safety

- Be aware of any source of flames, sparks, or heat (such as flames, heating coils, or hot plates) before working with any flammable substances.
- Know the location of lab fire extinguisher and fire-safety blankets.
- Know your school's fire-evacuation routes.
- If your clothing catches on fire, walk to the lab shower to put out the fire. Do not run.
- Never leave a hot plate unattended while it is turned on or while it is cooling.
- Use tongs or appropriate insulated holders when handling heated objects.
- Allow all equipment to cool before storing it.

Plant and Animal Safety

- Do not eat any part of a plant.
- Do not pick any wild plant unless your teacher instructs you to do so.
- Handle animals only as your teacher directs.
- Treat animals carefully and respectfully.
- Wash your hands throughly with soap and water after handling any plant or animal.

Cleanup

- Clean all work surfaces and protective equipment as directed by your teacher.
- Dispose of hazardous materials or sharp objects only as directed by your teacher.
- Wash your hands throughly with soap and water before you leave the lab or after any activity.

Student Safety Quiz

Circle the letter of the BEST answer.

1. Before starting an investigation or lab procedure, you should
   A. try an experiment of your own
   B. open all containers and packages
   C. read all directions and make sure you understand them
   D. handle all the equipment to become familiar with it

2. At the end of any activity you should
   A. wash your hands thoroughly with soap and water before leaving the lab
   B. cover your face with your hands
   C. put on your safety goggles
   D. leave hot plates switched on

3. If you get hurt or injured in any way, you should
   A. tell your teacher immediately
   B. find bandages or a first aid kit
   C. go to your principal's office
   D. get help after you finish the lab

4. If your glassware is chipped or broken, you should
   A. use it only for solid materials
   B. give it to your teacher for recycling or disposal
   C. put it back into the storage cabinet
   D. increase the damage so that it is obvious

5. If you have unused chemicals after finishing a procedure, you should
   A. pour them down a sink or drain
   B. mix them all together in a bucket
   C. put them back into their original containers
   D. dispose of them as directed by your teacher

6. If electrical equipment has a frayed cord, you should
   A. unplug the equipment by pulling the cord
   B. let the cord hang over the side of a counter or table
   C. tell your teacher about the problem immediately
   D. wrap tape around the cord to repair it

7. If you need to determine the odor of a chemical or a solution, you should
   A. use your hand to bring fumes from the container to your nose
   B. bring the container under your nose and inhale deeply
   C. tell your teacher immediately
   D. use odor-sensing equipment

8. When working with materials that might fly into the air and hurt someone's eye, you should wear
   A. goggles
   B. an apron
   C. gloves
   D. a hat

9. Before doing experiments involving a heat source, you should know the location of the
   A. door
   B. window
   C. fire extinguisher
   D. overhead lights

10. If you get chemicals in your eye you should
    A. wash your hands immediately
    B. put the lid back on the chemical container
    C. wait to see if your eye becomes irritated
    D. use the eyewash station right away, for a minimum of 15 minutes

Go online to view the Lab Safety Handbook for additional information.

Waves

Lesson 1 Introduction to Waves 4
Lesson 2 The Behavior of Mechanical Waves 22
Lesson 3 Light Waves 40
Lesson 4 The Behavior of Light Waves 60
Unit Review 81
Unit Performance Task 85

Dolphins are at home swimming through waves in the ocean. They communicate with each other using sound waves that travel through water or air. They can even use sound waves to find food.

Sound waves are only one of the many types of waves. You make water waves when you jump into a pool, and you use light waves to see everything around you. All of these waves share certain properties. Learning about the properties of waves can help you understand how musicians use instruments when playing in band, or how the satellites that send and collect information around Earth work. In this unit, you will explore waves and how wave behavior affects the world and the way you perceive it.

Why It Matters

Here are some questions to consider as you work through the unit. Can you answer any of the questions now? Revisit these questions at the end of the unit to apply what you discover.

Questions	Notes
How do people interact with waves in everyday life?	
Why can some waves, such as earthquake and tsunami waves, cause so much damage?	
Why do sound waves echo more in some locations than in others?	
How do devices send and receive information with radio waves?	
How does the way light waves interact with materials affect the way you perceive your surroundings?	
How can controlling the way light bends and reflects be used to help people?	

Unit Starter: Modeling Light and Sound

Light and sound waves travel through the air around you. They pass through some materials, but are blocked by others. These diagrams show sources of sound and light in a house.

The path of sound inside a house is modeled in this diagram by showing sound wave patterns from sources of sound, such as audio from a television.

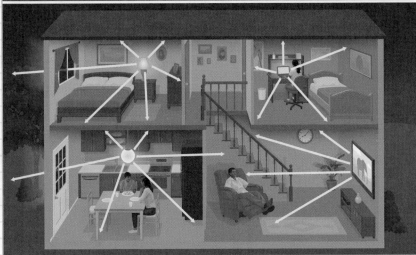

The path of light inside a house is modeled in this diagram by showing light wave patterns from sources of light, such as a lamp.

1. Think about your experiences with sound and light. What do these models show about how sound and light travel? Select all that apply.

    A. Light and sound travel away from their source.

    B. Light and sound are blocked by walls.

    C. Light is blocked by walls.

    D. Sound may be blocked by some walls and partially blocked by other walls.

Go online to download the Unit Project Worksheet to help you plan your project.

Unit Project

Design Wave Interactions

You may not be able to control the waves around you, but you may be able to control the way you interact with them. Choose one type of wave that you interact with, and design a structure or tool that changes the way the wave functions.

Introduction to Waves

Ocean waves can be described by the same properties as some other kinds of waves.

By the end of this lesson . . .

you will be able to model and discuss similarities and differences between waves you encounter every day.

Go online to view the digital version of the Hands-On Lab for this lesson and to download additional lab resources.

CAN YOU EXPLAIN IT?

Do falling dominoes form a wave?

Dominoes transfer energy much like a wave does. The person in the picture transferred energy from himself to the first domino. What will happen to the next domino and the ones after that?

1. Can you knock over the last domino without touching it? Sure, you can throw something at it. That's too easy! What is another way that you can knock over the last domino without touching it?

 EVIDENCE NOTEBOOK As you explore the lesson, gather evidence to help explain whether the domino example is similar to a wave.

Exploring Waves

Water crashing onshore, the spotlight on center stage, a siren blaring. These things may seem unrelated, but they have one thing in common—waves. The world is full of waves, including water, light, and sound waves. A **wave** is a repeating disturbance that transfers energy from one place to another.

These waves are the result of energy radiating outward from the person who jumped into the pool. The waves carry the energy through the water.

2. Think about the energy that was needed to form the wave in the pool. Where did the energy come from?

Waves Transfer Energy

A wave transfers energy in the direction that the wave travels. In the picture of the bug, the wave travels to the right, so energy is being transferred to the right. How much energy is transferred? That depends on the size of the disturbance. The greater the disturbance, the more energy is transferred. However, a wave does not transfer matter. The matter in which a wave travels does not move along with it.

Waves are quite varied and can be complex, but we can learn a lot from a simple wave. The rope wave on the next page shows energy being transferred in the direction the wave is traveling.

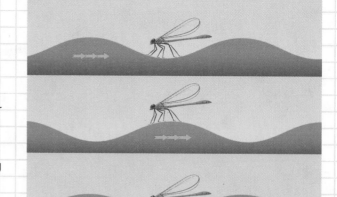

Waves on a pond move toward the shore, but the bug only bobs up and down due to a small disturbance.

Explore ONLINE!

3. Look at the wave that is made in the rope. The left end of the rope is being shaken, so the wave is traveling to the right / left. The energy of the wave travels to the right / left along the rope. As the wave goes by, each piece of the rope moves up and down / along with the wave.

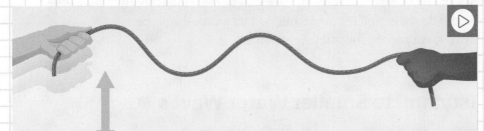

The points on the rope vibrate perpendicularly, or up and down, to the direction that the wave moves.

Waves Can Be a Pulse or a Repeating Movement

As a wave travels, energy is transferred. If the wave's energy is transferred one time only, then a wave *pulse* is formed. You can see the single pulse disturbance slow down as it moves through the medium. If the disturbance transfers energy in a repeating pattern, then a wave is formed. You can see the wave moving continuously.

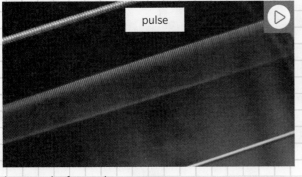

pulse

A wave pulse forms when energy is transferred one time.

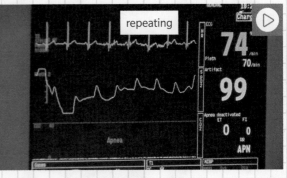

repeating

A wave forms when energy is transferred in a repeating pattern.

4. Discuss Together with a partner, look at the two photos and compare your observations. What wave patterns do you observe? Think about how they are similar and how they are different. Summarize your conclusions.

5. Do the dominoes from the beginning of the lesson exhibit any of the properties of waves discussed so far? List each of the properties. For each property, write a statement that begins, "Dominoes exhibit the property..." or "Dominoes do not exhibit the property..." and then state the property and record the evidence to support your statement.

Compare a Tsunami to Smaller Water Waves

Waves can be different sizes and shapes, and they can transfer different amounts of energy. A tsunami is a large ocean wave caused by a disturbance in or around the sea. It takes a great amount of energy to generate such a large wave. A tsunami can cause a lot of destruction once it reaches land.

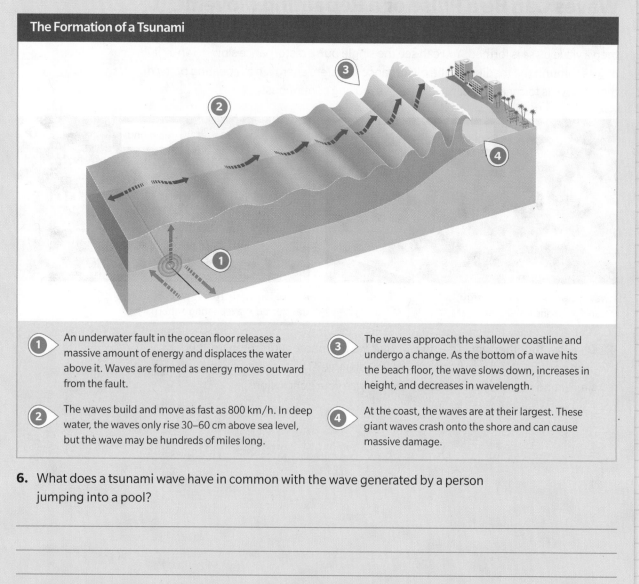

The Formation of a Tsunami

1. An underwater fault in the ocean floor releases a massive amount of energy and displaces the water above it. Waves are formed as energy moves outward from the fault.

2. The waves build and move as fast as 800 km/h. In deep water, the waves only rise 30–60 cm above sea level, but the wave may be hundreds of miles long.

3. The waves approach the shallower coastline and undergo a change. As the bottom of a wave hits the beach floor, the wave slows down, increases in height, and decreases in wavelength.

4. At the coast, the waves are at their largest. These giant waves crash onto the shore and can cause massive damage.

6. What does a tsunami wave have in common with the wave generated by a person jumping into a pool?

_____

_____

_____

_____

_____

_____

Comparing Longitudinal and Transverse Waves

As a wave travels through a medium, the particles of the medium move, or vibrate. Think back to the rope wave. If the wave is traveling to the right, which way are the pieces of rope moving? Up and down. The pieces of rope are the "particles" of the medium. In this case, the particles vibrate perpendicularly (up and down) to the direction the wave travels (to the right). This is an example of a *transverse wave*. In another type of wave, the particles vibrate parallel to the direction the wave travels. This is called a *longitudinal wave*. During an earthquake, both types of waves occur.

During an earthquake, the ground can move in dramatic ways. Powerful waves—both longitudinal and transverse waves—travel through Earth's crust.

7. Language SmArts Study the photo. What type of movement do you think is responsible for the damage shown? How could you relate the ground movement during an earthquake to wave type?

Hands-On Lab
Model Two Types of Waves

You will use a coiled spring toy to model two types of waves: a longitudinal wave and a transverse wave.

Procedure

STEP 1 Hold a coiled spring toy on the floor between you and a lab partner so that the spring is straight. This is the rest position of the spring. You and your lab partner should be facing each other. Another lab partner will document each step.

STEP 2 Move one end of the spring left and right at a constant rate. Record your observations for Wave 1.

Wave	Observations and Wave Types
Wave 1	
Wave 2	

STEP 3 Allow the spring to return to its rest position. Be sure you and the lab partner holding the other end of the spring are facing each other.

STEP 4 Push the spring toward your partner and then pull the spring backward repeatedly at a constant rate. Record your observations for Wave 2.

Analysis

STEP 5 **Discuss** Together with your partner, compare the waves you made. How are they alike? How are they different? What patterns did you observe? Include examples from your investigation.

Longitudinal and Transverse Waves

Both longitudinal waves and transverse waves transfer energy in the direction they travel. However, they differ in the way the disturbances move in relation to the direction of wave motion. In a longitudinal wave, the coils move parallel to the direction the wave travels. An area where the coils are close together is called a *compression*. An area where the coils are spread out is called a *rarefaction*. In a transverse wave, the coils move perpendicularly to the direction the wave travels. The highest point of the wave is called a *crest*, and the lowest point is called a *trough*.

There are other types of waves in the world. In fact, there is another kind of wave that is a combination of longitudinal waves and transverse waves. This is referred to as a *surface wave*. A ripple on a pond is an example of this combined wave type.

8. Label the type and parts of the waves shown here.

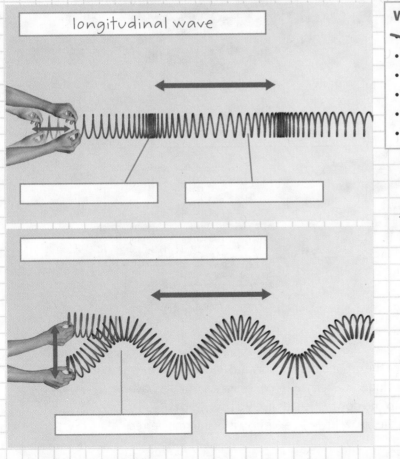

longitudinal wave

WORD BANK
- longitudinal wave
- transverse wave
- compression
- rarefaction
- crest
- trough

9. Remember the dominoes from the beginning of the lesson? Describe the movement of the collapsing dominoes as energy is transferred through them and then compare the movement of longitudinal waves to the movement of the dominoes. Record your evidence.

Analyze the Types of Waves in Earthquakes

Earthquakes produce both longitudinal waves and transverse waves. Both are types of *mechanical waves*, waves that transfer energy through a medium. Earthquake waves travel through Earth's crust. Longitudinal waves and transverse waves often travel at different speeds in a medium. During earthquakes, longitudinal waves are faster. They arrive first during an earthquake. Seconds later, the transverse waves arrive. These waves are slower but usually more destructive.

10. Based on what you learned in the modeling activity, label the two images below as an example of either a longitudinal wave or a transverse wave.

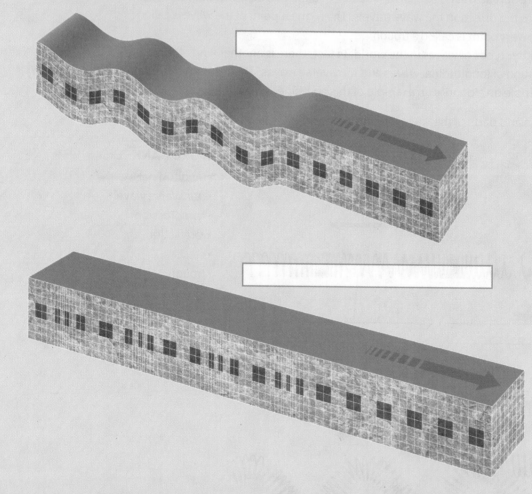

11. During an earthquake, if you see the ground moving forward and backward, then you are probably experiencing a longitudinal / transverse wave. If you see the ground moving up and down, then it's likely a longitudinal / transverse wave. In both cases, matter / energy is being transferred.

Identifying the Properties of Waves

Picture it: It's a calm day on a quiet street. Nobody is around. A car pulls up to the curb and parks. The driver gets out of the car, pulls down his hat to hide his face, and hurries away. Suddenly, the car explodes!

This is part of an exciting scene from a movie. The explosion created a blast wave. A high-pressure wave radiated out with great energy from the center of the explosion. Special effects experts carefully design and carry out these types of controlled explosions. All waves, including blast waves, have energy and amplitude. Amplitude is related to the amount of energy a wave carries. Special effects experts apply their knowledge of wave energy and amplitude to control the blast wave.

12. Why do you think the crew has suspended the cars by cables?

An explosion is a high-energy event that happens very quickly. A big part of a special effects team's job is ensuring the safety of people and the environment.

Properties of Waves Can Be Graphed

Waves are described by their properties. A measure of how far the particles in the medium move away from their normal rest position is the **amplitude**. Amplitude is half of the difference between the crest and the trough. The distance from any point on a wave to an identical point on the next wave is the **wavelength**. Wavelength measures the length of one cycle, or repetition, of a wave. Waves can be represented on a graph.

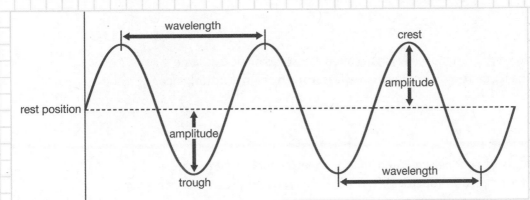

13. Discuss As a small group, discuss your observations of the image above. What amplitude and wavelength values could you read from the graph?

Hands-On Lab
Investigate Waves

You will investigate how mechanical waves in a water-filled tray affect the medium they pass through. Remember that a mechanical wave is a wave that travels through a medium.

Procedure and Analysis

STEP 1 Fill the tray about halfway with water. Place a cork in the water near the center of the tray.

STEP 2 Choose one group member to move the block up and down in the water at one end of the tray to create waves.

STEP 3 Observe the motion of the cork and the water. Sketch and describe your observations.

STEP 4 Do waves transfer energy or matter? Explain.

STEP 5 How could you test the following question: Do waves made by a large disturbance carry more energy than waves made by a small disturbance?

14. **Collaborate** With a partner, create an informational pamphlet that teaches a student how to graph the properties of a wave. You may use any wave source in your examples.

Frequency and Speed in a Wave

Think about making water waves again. The number of waves that you can make in five seconds depends on how quickly you move the block. The number of waves produced in a set amount of time is the **frequency** of the wave. Frequency is usually expressed in *hertz* (Hz). For waves, one hertz equals one wave per second (1 Hz = 1/s). The rate at which a wave travels is **wave speed**. It can be calculated by multiplying wavelength and frequency.

15. Do the Math The equation for wave speed (v) can be calculated using wavelength (λ) and frequency (f). For example, to determine the wave speed of a wave that has a wavelength of 5 m and a frequency of 4 Hz, replace the λ and f with the values given and solve: $v = 5 \text{ m} \times 4 \text{ Hz} = 20 \text{ m/s}$. What is the speed of a wave that has a wavelength of 2 m and a frequency of 6 Hz?

Energy and Amplitude in a Wave

The amplitude of a wave is dependent on energy. For example, when using a rope to make waves, you have to work harder to create a wave with a large amplitude than to create one with a small amplitude. It takes more energy to move the rope farther from its rest position. When comparing waves of the same frequency in the same medium, the energy of a wave is proportional to the amplitude of the wave squared. A wave with a large amplitude carries more energy than a wave with a small amplitude does.

Energy Is Proportional to Amplitude

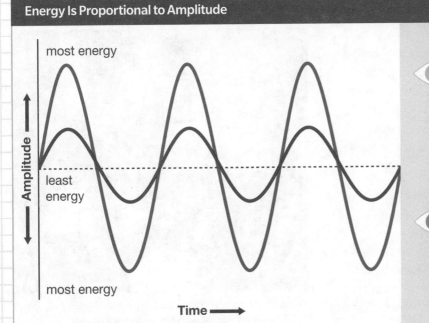

Lower amplitude waves are perfect for a fun day at the beach.

Surfers need higher amplitude waves to catch an exciting ride.

16. Engineer It An engineer has been asked to give advice about a wave pool at a local water park. The wave pool is generating waves that move too fast for the safety of park guests. Explain why the engineer suggested reducing the frequency of the wave generator.

Calculate Amplitude

The relationship between amplitude and wave energy states that energy is proportional to amplitude squared. For example, if the amplitude of the waves at one beach is three times the amplitude of the waves at another beach, you might think that the higher waves had three times as much energy as the smaller. However, it turns out that the higher waves would actually have nine times as much energy (because nine is three squared)! But what if we started by knowing energy instead? If your lab partner told you the energy of a wave had increased by a factor of 16, then how must the amplitude have changed? The amplitude must have quadrupled (because four is the square root of 16). If you know one variable, you can use the relationship between amplitude and energy to find the other variable.

 17. Do the Math Suppose the energy of a wave increased by a factor of 25. By what factor did the amplitude of the wave increase?

 Language SmArts

Apply Your Knowledge of Wave Energy and Amplitude

Think back to the movie scene where the car explodes. Special effects experts have to know how to keep people on the set safe during such dangerous scenes. An explosion produces a blast wave that radiates out with a lot of energy. Special effects experts apply their knowledge of wave energy and amplitude when designing a controlled explosion.

18. Special effects experts want the largest explosion that is safe for the people on set. Knowing that the energy of a wave is proportional to its amplitude squared helps them mathematically model the energy of the explosion and the amplitude of the blast wave. How does this knowledge help them determine where to place the actors and crew?

The special effects team is working hard to modify a vehicle for a special effect that will only last a few seconds.

_____

_____

_____

_____

_____

Continue Your Exploration

Name: _____   Date: _____

Check out the path below or go online to choose one of the other paths shown.

People in Science

- **Hands-On Labs** ✋
- **Earthquakes and Waves**
- **Propose Your Own Path**

Go online to choose one of these other paths.

James West, Research Scientist

James West's parents wanted him to be a medical doctor, but he wanted to study physics. His father was sure he'd never find a job that way. But West wanted to study what he loved. He did study physics, and he did find a job. He worked for Bell Laboratories and developed a microphone called the electret microphone. Today, West's microphone is in almost all telephones, cell phones, and other equipment that records sound.

West's interest in the microphone started with a question about hearing. A group of scientists wanted to know how close together two sounds could be before the ear would not be able to tell them apart. At the time, there was no microphone sensitive enough for their tests. West and fellow scientist Dr. Gerhard Sessler found that they could make a more sensitive microphone by using materials called electrets. The new microphones were cheaper, more reliable, smaller, and lighter than any microphone before.

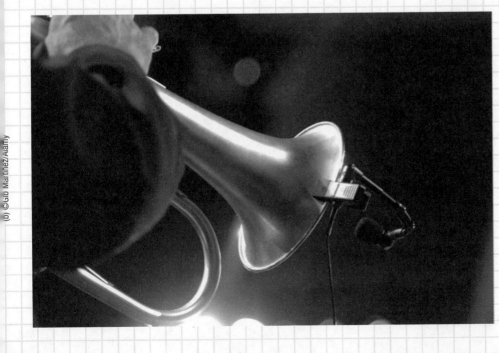

James West's research into sound waves and hearing has helped make microphones smaller.

Continue Your Exploration

1. James West has always been interested in how things work. When he was younger, he enjoyed taking apart small appliances to see what was inside. Why would curiosity about how things work be useful to an inventor?

2. Imagine yourself in the role of a research scientist. What would you find interesting or rewarding? What would you find difficult or challenging? Explain what you think it would be like to be a research scientist.

3. Research scientists work in all scientific disciplines. James West studied physics and focused his research around sound waves. Other research scientists study biology, geology, chemistry, or another science. If you were a research scientist, what discipline would you be most interested in studying and what specific topics would you be interested in focusing your research around? Explain why.

4. **Collaborate** Together with a partner, identify a scientist doing research related to waves. Generate a list of questions to ask the scientist. Work with your teacher to contact the scientist, then share your findings with your class.

Can You Explain It?

Name: _____ Date: _____

Do you remember comparing a row of collapsing dominoes to a wave?

Do falling dominoes form a wave?

 EVIDENCE NOTEBOOK
Refer to the notes in your Evidence Notebook to help you determine whether falling dominoes are a wave.

1. State your claim. Make sure your claim fully explains why or why not collapsing dominoes form a wave.

2. Summarize the evidence you have gathered to support your claim and explain your reasoning.

Checkpoints

Answer the following questions to check your understanding of the lesson.
Use the photo to answer Questions 3–5.

3. Look at the two waves shown in the diagram. Which property is different between the two waves?

   A. amplitude

   B. wave period

   C. frequency

   D. wavelength

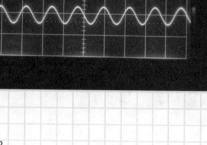

4. What types of wave patterns are shown? You may select more than one answer.

   A. repeating waves

   B. wave pulses

   C. transverse waves

   D. longitudinal waves

5. Look at the bottom waveform. How many wavelengths are shown?

   A. 2.5

   B. 4

   C. 8

   D. 16

Use the diagram to answer Question 6.

Explore
ONLINE!

6. Which statements are true about the diagram? Choose all that apply.

   A. The ball moves along with the wave as the wave moves.

   B. The ball moves up and down as the wave passes by.

   C. The wave transfers energy as it moves.

   D. The ball transfers energy to the wave.

Interactive Review

Complete this section to review the main concepts of the lesson.

A wave is a disturbance that transfers energy from one place to another. A wave transfers energy in the direction that it travels. Waves can travel as a single pulse or as a repeating series.

A. In your own words, describe what a wave is.

Waves can be classified by comparing the direction of the disturbance and the direction the wave travels.

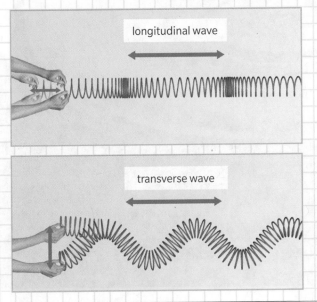

longitudinal wave

transverse wave

B. Explain the difference between longitudinal and transverse waves in terms of particle vibration.

Graphs can be used to represent waves. The key properties of waves include amplitude, wavelength, frequency, and wave speed. The energy of a wave is proportional to the amplitude of the wave squared.

C. Describe the wave in the image using what you know about the relationship between energy and amplitude in a wave.

The Behavior of Mechanical Waves

When a pool of water is disturbed, a wave spreads out over the surface of the water.

By the end of this lesson . . .

you will be able to explain how the behavior of mechanical waves relates to the medium that the waves travel through.

Go online to view the digital version of the Hands-On Lab for this lesson and to download additional lab resources.

CAN YOU EXPLAIN IT?

How can a map of the seafloor be generated using mechanical waves?

Depth (m): -1200, -1400, -1600, -1800, -2000, -2200, -2400, -2600

Humans and many other animals use light to see, but there are other ways to observe the world. Some animals, such as bats and dolphins, can also use mechanical sound waves to visualize the world around them. This image is a map of a seafloor that was created using mechanical waves.

1. How can mechanical waves be used to visualize an object?

EVIDENCE NOTEBOOK As you explore the lesson, gather evidence to help explain how mechanical waves can be used to generate a map of the seafloor.

Investigating Mechanical Waves

Waves, such as sound or ocean waves, are disturbances that carry energy from one place to another without permanently moving matter. When you shout at your friend across the room, sound waves carry energy through the air. Your friend senses that energy when he or she hears your voice. The air does not move from your vocal cords to your friend's eardrum, though. The sound waves move through the air, causing the air particles to vibrate as the energy passes through them.

2. Tsunamis are huge waves that carry large amounts of energy across the ocean. They are often caused by underwater earthquakes. Once a tsunami forms, the wave can travel hundreds of kilometers before reaching land. Are the water molecules that touch land the same ones that the earthquake initially moved? Why or why not?

The waves that can be seen moving through water are similar to sound waves in many ways.

Mechanical Waves

Many waves travel through a **medium**, a material through which the energy of the wave moves from one place to another. The medium can be air, water, steel, or any other material. A **mechanical wave** is a wave that travels through a medium due to the motion of matter. Sound is one common type of mechanical wave. When a book is slammed on a table, it creates a disturbance in the air particles around the book. This disturbance creates a wave that moves out from the book and reaches your ear. The air is the medium that the wave traveled through, and the sound is the mechanical wave.

3. Label the medium that each mechanical wave is passing through.

Medium

The characteristic that makes mechanical waves different from other types of waves is the need for a medium. A mechanical wave travels through a substance due to the physical motion of the medium itself. The waves in the wake of a boat occur when molecules of water move. The sound that you hear when a friend shouts occurs when air molecules move. An earthquake travels through the ground as the particles of rock and soil move up and down or back and forth. All of these materials are media, the plural of medium, that mechanical waves can move through.

Explore ONLINE!

Types of Mechanical Waves

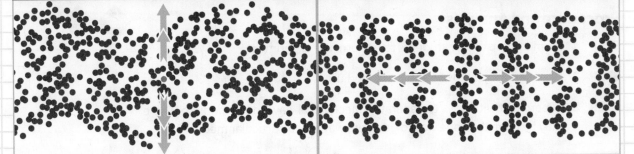

This is a transverse wave that travels from left to right. The particles move up and down as the wave travels to the right. This movement is similar to the way waves are commonly graphed.

This is a longitudinal wave that is traveling from left to right. The particles move right and left as the wave travels to the right. The peaks and troughs of the wave correspond to high and low concentrations of particles.

4. Which statement best describes how the particles of a medium behave when a mechanical wave moves through the medium?

A. Particles travel in the direction of the wave, away from the source of the wave.

B. Particles in the medium travel in the direction that is perpendicular to the motion of the wave.

C. Particles move as the wave passes them, but do not move along with the wave.

D. Particles stay in one place as the wave travels past them.

5. Language SmArts Split into small groups. Each group member should select a type of wave that they are familiar with. Determine where the initial energy for the wave comes from and what medium the wave travels through. Sketch the medium of the wave and the initial energy input. Taking turns, present each of your waves to the other members of your group.

Hands-On Lab
Generate Mechanical Waves

You will generate waves in several media and observe how the mechanical waves behave. Mechanical waves occur around you in many different ways. You can generate mechanical waves yourself by causing a disturbance in a medium. Think about the waves that you create every day and about the naturally occurring waves that you have observed.

MATERIALS
• long paper strips
• spring toys
• string or rope
• small tub of water

Procedure and Analysis

STEP 1 Form a group of four students to perform the experiment.

STEP 2 Choose an object to use as a wave medium.

STEP 3 Experiment with ways to generate a mechanical wave in the medium. There may be more than one way to generate waves in a particular medium.

STEP 4 Observe the waves that you generate and record your observations in the table below.

STEP 5 Repeat your explorations using other media.

Medium	Observations

EVIDENCE NOTEBOOK

6. What occurred when a wave moving through the water hit the side of its container? How might this relate to using waves in water to map the seafloor? Record your evidence.

STEP 6 Discuss Choose one of the media that you used to generate mechanical waves. With your group, identify how you can observe the amplitude, frequency, and speed of the wave as it travels through the medium.

Sound, Media, and Wave Speed

Some wave properties depend on the medium that the wave is traveling through. Each medium has properties that determine how its particles move. A **sound wave** is a mechanical wave caused by the vibration of particles as the wave travels through a medium. Sound waves can travel through solids, water, or gases. Because of this, sound waves can be used to observe how a medium affects a mechanical wave's properties.

Medium	State	Speed (m/s)
Argon	gas	323
Air	gas	343
Neon	gas	435
Ethanol	liquid	1162
Mercury	liquid	1450
Water	liquid	1482
Silver	solid	3650
Steel	solid	5200
Aluminum	solid	6420

Sound waves do not always travel at the same speed. The particles of different media interact in different ways. The speed of sound can change due to the arrangements and types of particles that the sound is traveling through.

 7. Do the Math What effect, if any, does the type of medium have on the speed of a sound wave?

    A. Sound travels at different speeds in different media, but there is no apparent pattern.

    B. The state of matter of the medium has a large effect on the speed of sound waves.

    C. The speed of sound depends on the medium and on the amplitude of the waves.

    D. The medium through which sound waves travel does not affect the speed of the waves.

Properties of Sound

Sound is a mechanical wave. All of the features of sound that you are familiar with are related to the properties of mechanical waves. The volume, or how loud something sounds, is directly related to the amplitude of a sound wave. If two sound waves are identical except for their amplitude, the sound wave with the higher amplitude will sound louder. Pitch, or how high or low a sound is, is directly related to frequency. If you hear a high-pitched buzz, it means the sound waves reaching your ear have a high frequency.

8. Choose a sound that you are familiar with. Describe how its features would relate to the properties of a mechanical wave.

Sound Waves

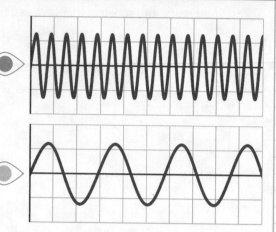

The sound wave shown has a high frequency and constant amplitude. The sound will have a high pitch and constant volume.

The sound wave shown has a low frequency and constant amplitude. The sound will have a low pitch and constant volume.

Identify Media

9. **Draw** When you listen to music from a musical instrument, how does the sound reach your ear? Using sketches, labels, and descriptions, show how the sound wave moves from the instrument, through air, toward a listener's ear. Be sure to describe any particle movement that occurs.

Analyzing Mechanical Waves and Energy

The amplitude of mechanical waves, like all other waves, depends on how much energy is carried by the waves. If two waves are identical in every way except for their amplitude, the wave with the greater amplitude will be carrying more energy.

Large earthquakes can occur as tectonic plates suddenly shift. In the area around this tectonic movement, the waves moving through the ground can be very destructive.

Farther away from the place where the initial disturbance occurred, the waves moving through the ground can still be felt, but are generally much less destructive.

10. Why might earthquakes be much more intense closer to the initial disturbance than they are further away?

Water Ripples

Explore ONLINE!

Ripples that move out from a disturbance in a pool of water are surface waves.

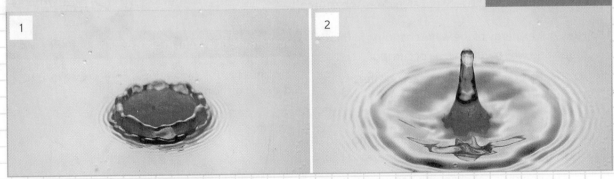

11. When the drop hits the water's surface, it generates a ripple. This ripple is known as a surface wave. What happens to the wave as it expands outward from the initial disturbance?

12. How does the diameter of each ripple change as time passes?

13. How does the amplitude of a ripple change as the ripple spreads out farther from the initial disturbance?

14. Discuss Since the ripple formed is a type of mechanical wave, what might the ripple's behavior indicate about how a mechanical wave moves through a medium?

Mechanical Waves Spread Out

Mechanical waves spread out through a medium over time. These waves generally spread out in as many directions as they are able. Surface waves on water spread out in a circle around the original disturbance. Sound waves in the air spread out as a sphere around the source of the sound. As a wave spreads out, energy is spread over a larger area. As a result the amount of energy in any one part of the wave also decreases. One reason that far-away sounds are so quiet is that less energy is reaching the listener. More energy will reach a listener who is one foot away from the sound's source than a listener who is twenty feet from the source.

Explore ONLINE!

15. How is the energy of the wave changing in this graph and why might this be occurring?

A. The energy is decreasing because the amplitude of the wave is decreasing.

B. The energy is not changing because the amplitude is constant although the frequency is changing.

C. The energy is not changing because the frequency is constant although the amplitude is changing.

D. The energy is decreasing because the frequency of the wave is decreasing.

Amplitude at a Point in Space

The amplitude of a water ripple will decrease as the diameter of the ripple increases.

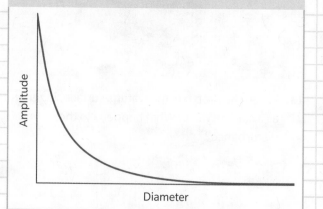

Absorption

Mechanical waves cause particles in a medium to move. As a wave passes through a medium, the medium's particles move. These particles bump into one another and transfer energy. During this movement, some of the wave's energy is converted to thermal energy by friction. *Absorption* refers to a medium converting the energy of a mechanical wave into other forms. When energy is absorbed by a medium, the medium gains thermal energy and the wave loses that energy.

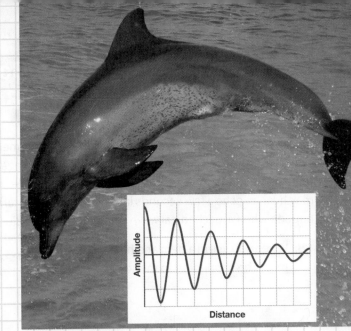

16. Whales and dolphins both use sound underwater. Dolphins use high-frequency sounds to locate objects. These waves can travel a few hundred meters. Whales use low-frequency sounds to communicate. These waves can travel hundreds of kilometers. Why might these sounds travel different distances?

Dolphins and whales make sounds that travel through water. As sound waves travel through water, they move water molecules. The graph above shows how the amplitude of a sound wave changes as it moves farther from the source of the sound.

_____

Absorption and Frequency

Absorption can vary based on the frequency of the wave. Generally, a high-frequency wave will lose more energy to absorption than a low-frequency wave. The more a particle is moved, the more energy it loses to friction. High-frequency waves move a medium's particles more often. The higher the frequency of the wave, the more energy it will lose to absorption. This is similar to what happens when you warm your hands using friction. Rubbing your hands against one another slowly will not generate much thermal energy. When you rub your hands quickly, the friction between them will generate a lot of thermal energy.

Analyze Sound Volume

17. Headphone earpieces can produce sounds that seem very loud to the listener. However, a person standing a meter away may not even be able to hear those same sounds. Why do these sounds seem so much quieter a short distance away?

_____

_____

_____

_____

_____

_____

Explaining the Behavior of Waves at Media Boundaries

Mechanical waves can travel through many different media, but they do not always move easily from one medium to another. Several things can occur when a wave reaches a boundary with a new medium. When you shout at a distant wall, you may hear an echo a few seconds later. An echo is an example of something that can happen when a mechanical wave contacts a new medium.

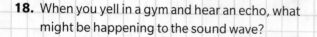

Explore ONLINE!

18. When you yell in a gym and hear an echo, what might be happening to the sound wave?

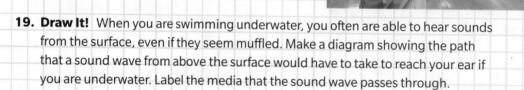

Echoes

19. Draw It! When you are swimming underwater, you often are able to hear sounds from the surface, even if they seem muffled. Make a diagram showing the path that a sound wave from above the surface would have to take to reach your ear if you are underwater. Label the media that the sound wave passes through.

20. What must have occurred for the sound to reach your ear?

Transmission

Consider what is happening when you hear sound through a wall. A sound wave traveled through the air, moved through the wall, and then traveled through air again to reach your ear. When a mechanical wave encounters a new medium, it can move into that new medium. This process is called *transmission*. On its path to your ear, the sound wave was transmitted from the air into the wall. When the sound wave traveled through the wall and encountered air, it was again transmitted to a new medium.

When a wave encounters a new medium, it is not always transmitted into the new medium.

21. What occurs when this wave traveling through the rope encounters a new medium, the wall?

Reflection

When a wave encounters the boundary of a medium, it does not always transmit into a new medium. Instead, the wave can reverse direction and travel back through the original medium. This behavior is known as reflection. When you hear sound echo off of a wall, the sound is reflecting. The wave encountered a new medium and was reflected.

Partial Reflection and Transmission ▷

When a wave encounters a new medium, it is normally partially transmitted and partially reflected.

22. How would you best describe the behavior of the wave when it reaches the boundary between the heavy particles and the light particles?

Partial Transmission and Reflection

Generally, when a mechanical wave encounters a boundary between two different media, the wave is not entirely reflected or transmitted. Some of the wave can be transmitted into the new medium. The remaining portion of the wave is reflected back into the original medium. This is why you can hear the sounds of a basketball game from outside a gym, even though there may be echoes inside the gym as well.

Amplitude and Energy in Partial Reflection

Explore
ONLINE!

Remember that a wave's frequency does not depend on the medium it is traveling through.

23. What do you notice about the amplitude of the reflected wave?

Energy In Partially Reflected Waves

When a mechanical wave is partially reflected and partially transmitted, the original wave becomes two waves. The energy from the original wave is split between the transmitted wave and the reflected wave. Because the original wave's energy is split between the two new waves, each of the new waves will have less energy than the original wave. Amplitude depends on the medium, so the transmitted wave's amplitude could be very different. The reflected wave and the original wave both move through the same medium, so they can be directly compared.

Engineer It
Explore Mechanical Waves in Medicine

24. Doctors use ultrasound, or high-frequency sound that humans cannot hear, to generate images of the inside of a person's body. Waves are sent through the body, bounce off of organs, and then return to the imaging device. How are reflection and transmission of ultrasonic waves used to produce this image?

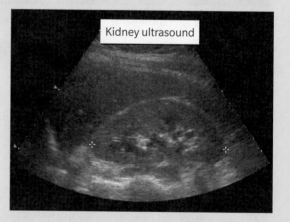
Kidney ultrasound

_____

_____

_____

_____

_____

EVIDENCE NOTEBOOK

25. Ultrasounds use reflection and transmission to generate an image from waves. How might these same principles be used to map a seafloor? Record your evidence.

Continue Your Exploration

Name: _____   Date: _____

Check out the path below or go online to choose one of the other paths shown.

Designing Soundproof Rooms

- **Hands-On Labs** ✋
- **Engineering to Prevent Earthquake Damage**
- **Propose Your Own Path**

Go online to choose one of these other paths.

When engineers design recording studios or practice spaces for musicians, they carefully consider ways to make the rooms ideal at handling loud sounds. Typically, they design the rooms to address several problems. These problems include echoes inside the room that make it hard to hear the desired sound and sounds that are loud enough that they can even be heard outside of the room.

1. Categorize the wave phenomena by the music studio problem that they relate to. Each problem may have more than one wave phenomena associated with it.

   Echoes _____

   Sound audible in other rooms _____

WORD BANK
- absorption
- reflection
- transmission

Continue Your Exploration

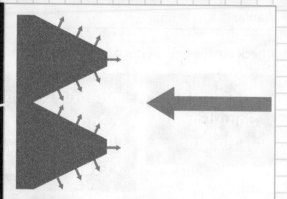

Acoustic panels are designed to eliminate echoes in a room. The shape of acoustic panels changes how sound bounces off of a wall or ceiling. Instead of bouncing right back, the sound bounces in many directions. When a sound wave is split up in this way, the sound does not echo.

2. Acoustic panels are designed to solve problems related to the _____ of sound in a music studio. Choose one.

   A. absorption

   B. reflection

   C. transmission

3. Music practice spaces often have very thick walls made of dense materials such as cement. A sound wave moving through one of these walls moves a lot of particles and loses energy. What sound phenomenon are architects making use of with these walls? Explain your reasoning.

4. **Collaborate** With a partner, discuss ways in which the room you are currently in is or is not soundproofed. Consider ways that you could modify the room to better keep sound from escaping out of the room.

Can You Explain It?

Name: **Date:**

Take another look at the seafloor map that was generated using mechanical waves.

How can a map of the seafloor be generated using mechanical waves?

EVIDENCE NOTEBOOK

Refer to the notes in your Evidence Notebook to help you construct an explanation of how a seafloor could be mapped using mechanical waves.

1. State your claim. Make sure your claim fully explains how a seafloor map can be generated using mechanical waves.

2. Summarize the evidence you have gathered to support your claim and explain your reasoning.

Checkpoints

Answer the following questions to check your understanding of the lesson.

Use the illustration to answer Question 3.

3. This image shows what happened after a wave traveling from the left encountered a boundary between its original medium and another, less dense medium. What happened at the boundary between media? Choose all that apply.

   A. Some of the wave's energy was transmitted to the less dense medium.

   B. Part of the wave was reflected back into the original medium.

   C. The transmitted part of the wave carried particles from one medium to the other.

---

4. Sound is made up of electromagnetic / mechanical waves that travel through a medium. As the sound wave travels through a medium, it moves particles in that medium permanently / temporarily. When the sound wave strikes a boundary between air and water, it will generally be completely / partially reflected.

Use the illustration to answer Questions 5 and 6.

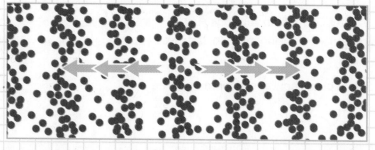

5. This illustration represents a sound wave traveling from left to right. As the wave passes the location of the particle represented by the red dot, how does the particle move?

   A. The particle travels from left to right along with the sound wave.

   B. The particle vibrates horizontally, moving both left and right.

   C. The particle vibrates vertically, moving both up and down.

6. As this sound wave spreads through the air, it moves the air particles smaller and smaller distances. What causes this change in the amount of motion? Choose all that apply.

   A. Amplitude decreases as the energy of a wave spreads across a greater amount of the medium.

   B. Amplitude decreases as medium's particles move away from the sound's source.

   C. Amplitude decreases as friction removes energy from the sound wave.

Interactive Review

Complete this interactive study guide to review the lesson.

Mechanical waves occur when energy moves through a medium due to the motion of particles. The particles move as the wave passes through them, but they do not move with the wave.

A. When a mechanical wave travels through a medium, how does the wave affect the medium's particles?

As a mechanical wave travels through a medium, its amplitude can decrease due to the wave being spread across more matter and energy being transformed into other forms.

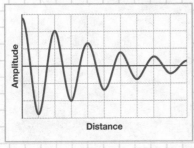

B. Describe why a sound wave's amplitude might decrease as it moves through a medium.

When a mechanical wave reaches a boundary between two media, the wave can be reflected, transmitted, or undergo a combination of reflection and transmission.

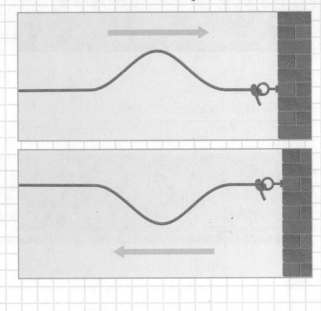

C. When a mechanical wave encounters a new medium, it may be partially reflected and partially transmitted. Describe how the properties of the original wave will change as it is transmitted through the new medium.

Light Waves

Light streams into this space. Some areas are brightly lit while other areas remain in shadow. What else do you observe?

By the end of this lesson . . .

you will be able to use models to describe light waves and compare them to mechanical waves.

Go online to view the digital version of the Hands-On Lab for this lesson and to download additional lab resources.

CAN YOU EXPLAIN IT?

What characteristics of light allow for the colorful display of a sunrise or sunset?

Light from the sun illuminates Earth.

1. That sun is bright! How did that sunlight reach us all the way here on Earth? Light from the sun travels through the vacuum of space to Earth as transverse waves. These transverse waves do not need a medium in which to travel. Think about the path that light from the sun takes to shine through your window. What media does it travel through?

EVIDENCE NOTEBOOK As you explore the lesson, gather evidence to help explain how light waves produce the colors we see in the sky.

Exploring the Nature of Light

A light bulb, a burning log, a candle—these are all sources of light. **Light** is a type of energy that travels as waves. Even living things such as fireflies and some fish that live in the ocean produce light. The most important source of light for life on Earth is the sun. Light is different from other kinds of wave. Other kinds of waves, like sound waves and water waves, must travel through matter. Light does not require matter through which to travel. Light is an *electromagnetic wave*.

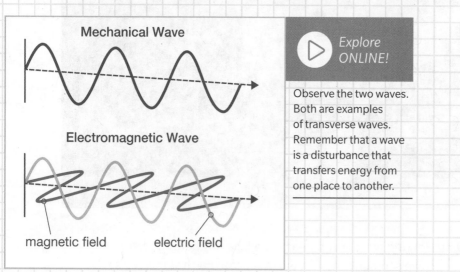

Explore ONLINE!

Observe the two waves. Both are examples of transverse waves. Remember that a wave is a disturbance that transfers energy from one place to another.

2. **Discuss** Together with a partner, compare the two waves. What patterns do you observe? How are the two waves similar? How are they different?

Electromagnetic Waves

As the word *electromagnetic (EM)* suggests, these waves have two parts. They are made up of changing electric and magnetic fields. When an electrically charged particle vibrates, it disturbs the electric and magnetic fields around it. These two vibrating fields produce EM waves. The fields are perpendicular to each other and carry energy away from the charged particle. Because electric and magnetic fields can exist in empty space, EM waves do not need a medium in which to travel.

Electromagnetic Spectrum

Look around you. You can see things that reflect light to your eyes. Light that we readily see is called *visible light*. It is essential for human vision. If a bee was in the room, the bee might see things differently than you do. This is because bees can see a kind of light—called *ultraviolet light*—that you can't see. Both ultraviolet light and visible light are part of a larger range of waves known as the *electromagnetic (EM) spectrum*. The EM spectrum is composed of many different types of EM waves, including X rays, radio waves, and microwaves.

The Electromagnetic Spectrum

The regions in the electromagnetic spectrum have different frequencies and wavelengths.

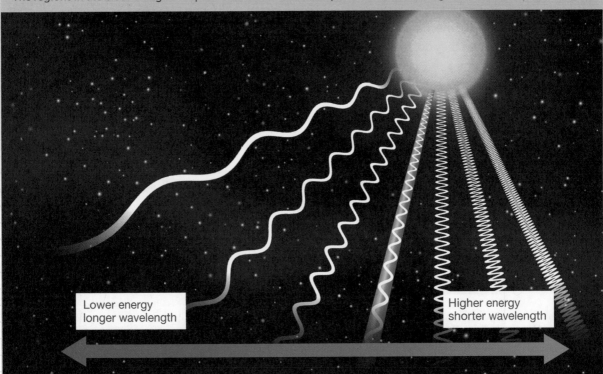

Lower energy longer wavelength

Higher energy shorter wavelength

Radio waves have frequencies less than about 3×10^{11} Hz.

Microwaves have frequencies of about $1.6 \times 10^9 - 3 \times 10^{10}$ Hz.

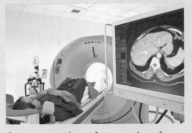

Millimeter waves have frequencies of about $3 \times 10^{10} - 10^{12}$ Hz.

Infrared waves have frequencies of about $10^{12} - 10^{14}$ Hz.

Visible light waves have frequencies of about $4 \times 10^{14} - 8 \times 10^{14}$ Hz.

Ultraviolet waves have frequencies of about $10^{15} - 10^{17}$ Hz.

X-rays have frequencies of about $10^{17} - 10^{20}$ Hz.

Gamma rays have frequencies of about 10^{20} Hz $- 10^{21}$ Hz.

Cosmic rays have frequencies greater than 10^{21} Hz.

Speed of Light

In a vacuum, all EM waves, including light, move at the same speed: 300,000,000 meters/second. This is called the speed of light, and it is constant. Although EM waves do not need a medium like mechanical waves do, EM waves can travel through many different materials. When they do, they travel more slowly than they do in a vacuum.

3. **Do the Math** The speed of light in a vacuum is 300,000,000 meters/second. As light travels through a medium, it interacts with the particles of the medium and slows down. Light travels only three-fourths as fast in water as in a vacuum. It travels about two-thirds as fast in glass and about two-fifths as fast in diamond. Select the correct speed of light for each medium below.

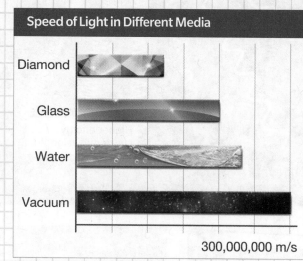

Speed of Light in Different Media

Diamond

Glass

Water

Vacuum

300,000,000 m/s

A. In diamond: 120,000,000 / 200,000,000 meters/second

B. In glass: 200,000,000 / 225,000,000 meters/second

C. In water: 200,000,000 / 225,000,000 meters/second

Energy and Frequency

What does the energy of an EM wave depend upon? It depends on the wave's frequency. High-frequency, short-wavelength EM waves have more energy than low-frequency, long-wavelength waves. The more energy EM waves have, the more dangerous they can be to living tissue. For example, x-rays have very high frequencies and carry a lot of energy. When working with x-rays, special precautions must be taken, such as wearing a lead apron to block most of the rays. In contrast, radio waves, which have very low frequencies and carry less energy, are much safer. They are used often, such as in walkie-talkies and baby monitors.

EVIDENCE NOTEBOOK

4. How is the structure of light waves similar to other waves that you have studied? How is the structure different? How do light waves differ from other EM waves? Record your evidence.

The Atmosphere Blocks Some EM Radiation

The sun gives off some radiation in every part of the EM spectrum. However, the atmosphere blocks most of the higher-energy radiation, such as x-rays and gamma waves, so they don't reach ground level. Radio waves, visible light, and some UV waves do reach the ground.

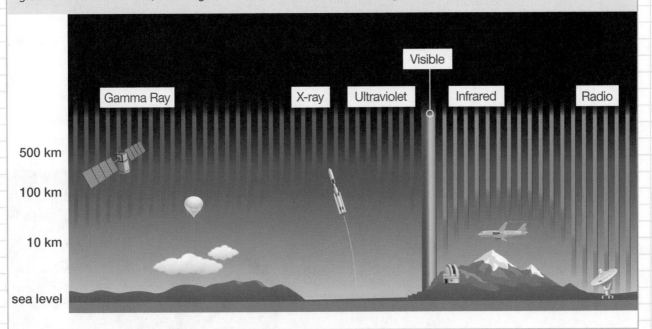

5. **Language SmArts** Why do you think the best ground-based telescopes are radio telescopes? Develop your claim by providing strong, logical reasons and evidence.

You can see in the diagram above that not all wavelengths of light pass through the atmosphere equally. Notice that most of the visible light and and a "window" of radio frequencies are able to pass through the atmosphere to ground level. Fortunately, the atmosphere blocks most of the higher-frequency EM waves from reaching the Earth's surface. One of these higher-frequency waves is ultraviolet (UV) light. Small amounts of UV light are good for your body. Skin cells that are exposed to UV light produce vitamin D. This vitamin helps our intestines absorb calcium. Calcium helps to produce strong teeth and bones. Have you heard the saying, "too much of a good thing can be bad?" This saying is true for UV light. Too much UV light can lead to a painful sunburn. Continued long-term exposure to UV light can result in wrinkles, eye damage, or even skin cancer. Protecting ourselves from over-exposure to UV light is pretty easy. You can use a sunscreen with a high SPF (sun protection factor) or wear protective clothing. Remember that UV light is present on cold days and can travel through clouds.

6. **Collaborate** Together with a partner, create an informative poster or brochure about ultraviolet light. Include both the good effects and the bad effects of UV light.

7. Engineer It When designing devices, engineers need to understand what makes some EM waves safe and others potentially dangerous. Engineers know that the safety of EM waves has to do with their frequency and the energy they carry. More energy means ~~higher~~ / Lower frequency. Higher frequency means more / ~~less~~ danger to human cells. Radio waves are safe / ~~not safe~~ for humans. They are an example of high-frequency / ~~low-frequency~~ radiation. Ultraviolet light, though, has a higher / ~~lower~~ frequency, and it is ~~not at all~~ / possibly dangerous to human cells.

Compare Sound Waves and Light Waves

One main difference between sound waves and light waves is the media in which they can travel. Mechanical waves, such as sound waves, cannot travel without a medium. On the other hand, EM waves, such as light waves, can travel with or without a medium.

▷ *Explore ONLINE!*

In this demonstration, tubing is connected to a pump that is removing air from the jar. As the air is removed, the buzzing timer sounds quieter and quieter.

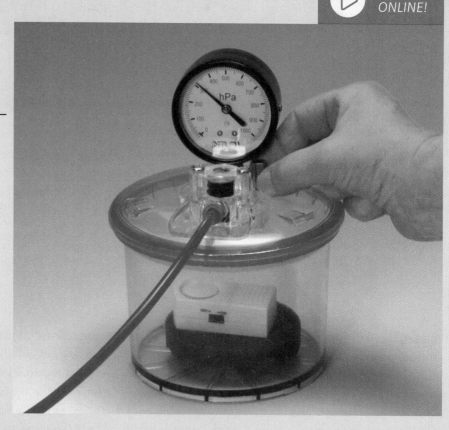

8. What do you observe in the photo above? What could you infer from your observations? Select all choices that apply.

   A. I could see the bell after the air was removed from the chamber.

   B. I could hear the bell after the air was removed from the chamber.

   C. This demonstration shows that light can travel through a vacuum, but sound cannot.

   D. This demonstration shows that both light and sound can travel through a vacuum.

Analyzing Human Perception of Light Waves

Have you heard of ROY G. BiV? Many students are taught to remember the colors of the rainbow by using this mnemonic device, which stands for *red, orange, yellow, green, blue,* and *violet*. Have you ever wondered why rainbows always follow this pattern?

A rainbow can appear in unexpected places.

9. Where have you seen rainbows? How do those rainbows compare to the image above? What do rainbows have to do with visible light?

Frequency, Wavelength, Amplitude, and Color

Imagine you had a machine that let you change the variables in the visible spectrum to see how they affect the color of light. Examine these images to see some possible results.

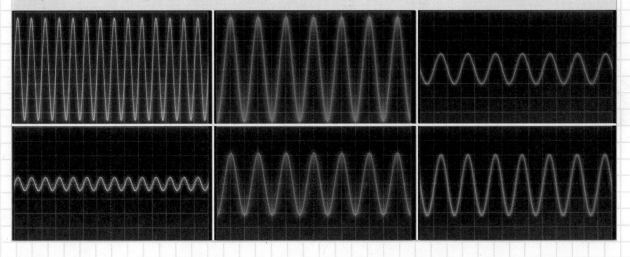

10. Do the Math As you just observed, you can change the frequency, wavelength, and amplitude of a wave. As the wavelength increases, frequency increases / decreases. This means that wavelength and frequency are directly / inversely proportional. Changing either of these properties changed / did not change the amplitude.

Light Waves and Color

Light travels as waves, which are usually invisible to us because their wavelengths are too short or too long for the human eye to see. However, waves in the visible range appear to us as a spectrum of colors. Each color corresponds to a certain wavelength (or frequency) of light. Our eyes interpret these different wavelengths as different colors. For example, blue light has a wavelength of about 475 nanometers, while red light has a wavelength of about 650 nanometers.

White light is what we perceive when our eyes detect all wavelengths of visible light at once in equal proportions. Sunlight contains all wavelengths of visible light.

What determines the color of light? The wavelength (or frequency) of light determines its color. The shortest wavelengths of light are seen as violet, and the longest wavelengths are seen as red. We see this separation of light by wavelength when light shines through a prism to reveal the different colors of the rainbow.

Light Traveling Through a Prism

Direction of light wave →

11. Based on your observations of the prism, select the true statements.

A. When light travels through a prism, the light is separated by wavelength.

B. Humans see the different wavelengths of visible light as different colors.

C. The prism is being used to combine different colors of light.

D. The light bends when it enters the prism and again when it leaves the prism.

Light Waves and the Perception of Color

Color is everywhere in nature. The arrows in the image below represent the wavelengths of light of the main colors that humans can see. Compare how the incoming colors of light behave when they encounter the kitten's black fur, its white fur, the green grass, and the yellow dandelion.

What happens to light when it hits an object? Some of the colors of light can reflect off the object, while others can be absorbed by the object. Reflection is the bouncing of light off a surface. Absorption is when light enters matter and does not leave it. Grass, for example, reflects green light while absorbing other colors of light. When you look at the grass, that green light enters your eyes, so the grass appears green.

12. **Draw** In the space below, draw a model to illustrate why an apple looks red and a nearby banana looks yellow.

 EVIDENCE NOTEBOOK

    13. How does the color of sunlight contribute to the colors of a sunrise or a sunset? What other characteristics of light waves are involved in the display of colors?

Available Light and the Perception of Color

The campfire is bright, and you can see the colors of the people's clothing very well.

This area is partially lit, so the grass may appear a duller green than it actually is.

There's almost no light in this area far away from the campfire or light in the tent. You can't see any colors. Why? Because there's not enough light to be reflected back to your eyes!

14. If visible light includes a range of colors, what determines the color of an object?

    A. The colors the object reflects and absorbs

    B. The size and shape of the object

    C. The light that is available in the area

    D. The texture of the object

Analyze Available Light

An object's appearance depends in part on the light that is available in the area. The light source can make a big difference in what you see!

15. Compare the color and amount of light in the day and night scenes. Support your conclusions.

_____

_____

_____

_____

_____

_____

_____

Investigating Light as Transverse Waves

We've learned that light waves are transverse waves. As in all transverse waves, the highest points on a light wave are called crests, and the lowest points are called troughs. The amplitude of a wave is the distance from the normal rest position to a crest or a trough. For all waves, the amplitude of a wave is related to its energy—for light waves, the greater the amplitude, the brighter the light. Brightness is measured in lumens.

Brightness Versus Distance

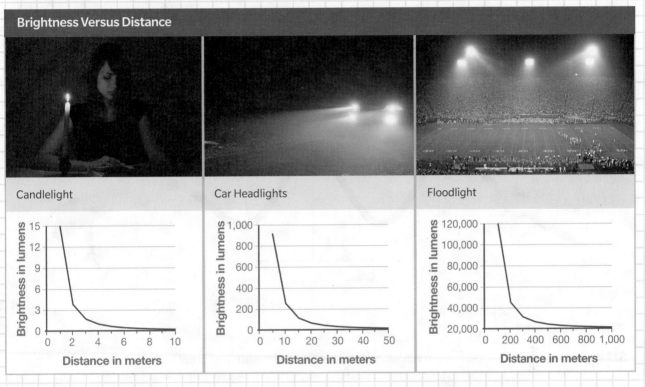

Candlelight

Car Headlights

Floodlight

16. What happens to the amplitude of a light wave as it travels away from the source?

17. **Discuss** Together with a partner, analyze the photos and the graphs to draw evidence-based conclusions about the energy, amplitude, and brightness of light. Review your analysis to relate the energy of a light wave to what we see as we get farther away from a light source.

Model Specific Wave Properties

You will make observations about the relationship between energy and amplitude in a mechanical wave and then relate your findings to the brightness of light.

STEP 1 Let's review the properties of a wave. Add labels to the parts of the wave moving through the rope in the diagram.

MATERIALS
- masking tape
- rope, 2 meters
- tape measure, 1.5 meters

WORD BANK
~~amplitude~~
wavelength
trough
crest

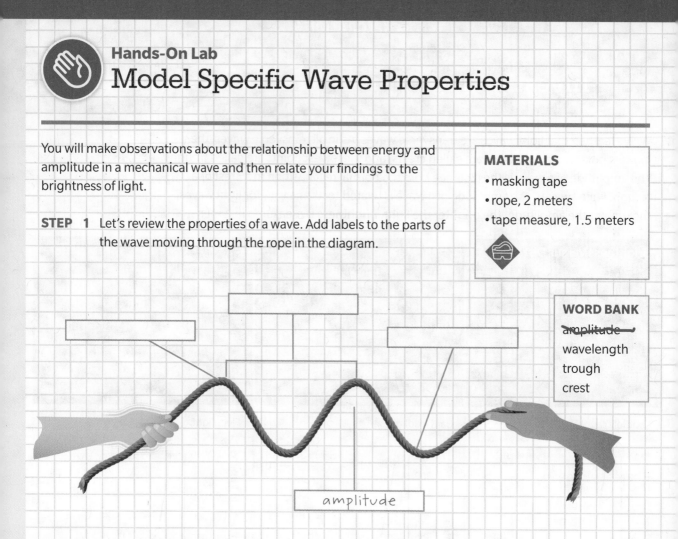

amplitude

Procedure

STEP 2 You will use a rope to form waveforms of specific wavelength and amplitude. Work with your group to determine the best way to make and record waves with a rope.

STEP 3 Think about how you will control the rope to get the correct wavelength and amplitude. How will you measure the wave properties to show that you've reached the correct values? How will you record your waveforms?

STEP 4 Record your proposed procedure. Sketch your proposed setup.

STEP 5 See the table below for the four waveforms you will make and record.

Wavelength (cm)	Amplitude (cm)	Waveform
40	10	
60	10	
40	30	
60	30	

Analysis

STEP 6 Analyze the relationship between a wave's wavelength and amplitude and the energy required to make the wave. What observations do you have from the activity?

    A. More energy is required to make a waveform of larger amplitude.

    B. About the same energy is required to make a waveform of any wavelength.

    C. Less energy is required to make a waveform of smaller amplitude.

    D. About the same energy is required to make a waveform of any amplitude.

STEP 7 What are your conclusions about the relationship between amplitude and energy for the waveforms you made? Use data to support your conclusions.

Your findings with the mechanical waves can be related to light waves, particularly their brightness. More energy was needed to make a rope wave of larger amplitude. Similarly, the larger the amplitude of a light wave is, the more energy it carries. The energy of the light wave is proportional to its amplitude squared. This greater energy is, in turn, related to a greater perceived brightness of the light.

18. Draw Use the space below or draw on a piece of paper. How do rope waves relate to light waves? Think about the relationship between a wave's energy and amplitude. Also think about the relationship between energy and brightness in light waves. Draw two waves, one with a smaller amplitude and one with a larger amplitude. Then, illustrate each amplitude in terms of light.

Investigate the Brightness of Light

The brightness of light allows you to see things clearly—or makes them fade away. Applying knowledge about the brightness of light can even save you money.

19. A normal light bulb has just two settings: "on" or "off." However, a 3-level incandescent light bulb is more flexible. It has three "on" settings: low, medium, and high. The brightness of the light from the bulb can be changed by adjusting the amount of electricity it uses. The three levels of brightness are usually described by the terms *watts* and *lumens*. The watts unit is related to the amount of electricity (energy) something uses. The lumens unit is related to the brightness of light. A particular bulb is brighter when it uses more energy. Look at the table below. Write the correct lumens values from the word bank to complete the table.

WORD BANK
305 lumens
995 lumens
1300 lumens

3-Level Incandescent Light Bulb	Level 1	Level 2	Level 3
Energy	30 watts	70 watts	100 watts
Brightness			

20. You can save money by using just the right amount of light for a task. Which of the following are efficient uses of light for the task described? Use the information in the table to help you.

   A. Use level 1 as background light when friends drop by for movie night.

   B. Use level 3 while lounging and watching TV with the family.

   C. Use level 2 in the kitchen when preparing a sandwich.

   D. Use level 3 when sculpting fine details in a piece of clay for art class.

Continue Your Exploration

Name: _____ Date: _____

Check out the path below or go online to choose one of the other paths shown.

| What Color Should the Doghouse Be? | • Hands-On Labs ✋
• How Can Light Help Navigation?
• Propose Your Own Path | *Go online to choose one of these other paths.* |

Reflection and Absorption

Light energy that is not reflected by an object is absorbed or transmitted. When light energy is absorbed, it is converted into thermal energy. Combine this information with what you have learned about perceived color to determine which color to paint some doghouses.

1. What color do you predict will work better in warmer climates? What color do you predict will work better in cooler climates? Why?

Continue Your Exploration

Light Reflectance Value (LRV) is a measurement that tells you how much light a color reflects. From that value, you can infer how much light the color absorbs. Designers and painters often use LRV in their work. The following table shows the LRV of the paint colors available to paint the doghouses.

Available Paint Colors		
Perceived color	Name of color	LRV
	Rosebud	62.26
	Crimson	12.35
	Sky	62.66
	Midnight	4.51
	Mint	74.93
	Forest	8.79

2. Which color has the highest LRV?

3. Which color has the lowest LRV?

4. Which colors would you recommend for doghouses built in warmer climates? Support your answer with evidence.

5. Which colors would you recommend for doghouses built in cooler climates? Support your answer with evidence.

6. Collaborate In a small group, list at least eight common car colors. Use a Venn diagram to sort the colors by "good in hot weather" and "good in cold weather." The colors that overlap are good for both hot and cold. Share your results with the class.

Can You Explain It?

Name: Date:

Consider again the light waves given off by the sun and other sources of light.

> **What characteristics of light allow for the colorful display of a sunrise or sunset?**
>
>

EVIDENCE NOTEBOOK
Refer to the notes in your Evidence Notebook to help you determine how light waves produce the colors we see in the sky.

1. State your claim. Make sure your claim fully explains the phenomenon.

2. Summarize the evidence you have gathered to support your claim and explain your reasoning.

Checkpoints

Answer the following questions to check your understanding of the lesson.

3. You walk into a room and see a black-colored orange on a table. Which of the following factors most likely affected your perception of the orange's color? Select all that apply.

   A. Only white light is available in the area of the orange.

   B. Only blue light is available in the area of the orange.

   C. Blue light is being absorbed by the orange.

   D. Blue light is reflecting off the orange.

Use the diagram to answer Question 4.

4. Study the diagram. Which statements are true? Choose all that apply.

   A. Light travels at the same speed in water, glass, and diamond.

   B. Light travels the fastest in a vacuum compared to the other mediums.

   C. Light can't travel through any mediums at all.

   D. Light travels slower in mediums than it does in a vacuum.

   E. Light can travel with or without a medium.

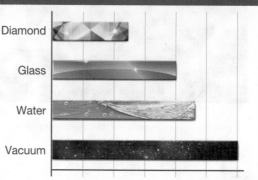

Speed of Light

Diamond

Glass

Water

Vacuum

300,000,000 m/s

Use the photos to answer Question 5.

5. Observe the photos. The main difference between the photos is the wavelength / brightness / frequency of the light being shown, which is related to the amplitude / length / color of the light. The amplitude of the brighter light is greater than / less than the amplitude of the dimmer light. What about the energy of the lights? The energy of the brighter light is greater than / less than the amplitude of the dimmer light.

6. The color with the shortest wavelength is violet. Violet has the highest / lowest frequencies. The various wavelengths of light can be split / combined to produce white light. Ultraviolet, or UV, light has slightly shorter / longer wavelengths than violet light.

Interactive Review

Complete this section to review the main concepts of the lesson.

Light waves are electromagnetic (EM) waves, which are caused by disturbances in electric and magnetic fields. An EM wave can travel through matter or empty space.

A. How are the parts of the EM spectrum different from each other?

The color of light is determined by the wavelength (or frequency) of light. The perceived color of an object is determined by the colors of light reflected by the object.

B. How does the amount of light affect the perceived color of an object?

The amplitude of a light wave is related to the energy of the wave and the perceived brightness of the light.

C. How is the amplitude and energy of a light wave related to its frequency and wavelength?

The Behavior of Light Waves

On a rainy night in the city, light shines brightly in interesting ways from the buildings, the water, and the camera lens.

By the end of this lesson . . .

you will be able to describe how light waves interact with different media and explain how devices are designed to use light waves.

Go online to view the digital version of the Hands-On Lab for this lesson and to download additional lab resources.

CAN YOU EXPLAIN IT?

Why does the same room lit with the same flashlight look different in these photos?

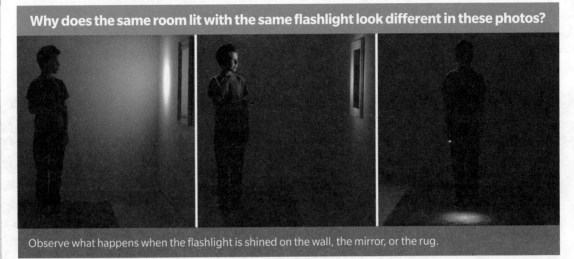

Observe what happens when the flashlight is shined on the wall, the mirror, or the rug.

1. Compare the photos above. In each picture, the light source is the flashlight held by the boy. Evaluate the amount and quality of light in each picture. What could explain how the same light source in the same room can produce such different results?

EVIDENCE NOTEBOOK As you explore the lesson, gather evidence to help explain how the behavior of light affects what we see and how we see it.

Exploring Interactions of Light and Matter

Interactions between light and matter produce many common but spectacular effects, such as rainbows and optical illusions. Light, like other electromagnetic waves, can travel through empty space, but when light encounters a material, it can interact with the material in several ways. These interactions play an important role in how people see light.

2. What do you observe in the photo? Why do you think light behaves in this way?

Matter Can Transmit Light

Look at the wrapped sandwiches. How do they differ? Why can't you see all three sandwiches beneath the wrappers equally well? The reason is how light interacts with matter. Different amounts of light pass through the different wrappers.

Light and other electromagnetic waves travel from a source in all directions, and they can travel through empty space or through matter. The passing of light waves through matter is called **transmission**. The medium through which light passes can transmit all, some, or none of the light. As you can see in the photos, the clear plastic wrap transmits all of the light, so we can clearly see the sandwich inside. When light travels through the waxed paper, only some of the light is transmitted. That sandwich is visible, but it looks fuzzy. The brown paper transmits none of the light, and the result is that we can't see the sandwich within it at all.

These sandwiches are wrapped in clear plastic wrap, waxed paper, or brown paper. How do the different wrappers affect what we see?

Transmission and Absorption of Light

The clear plastic wrap around the first sandwich is an example of a transparent material. *Transparent* materials transmit light straight through, and objects can be seen clearly through them. Clean air and clean water are also transparent. *Translucent* materials transmit light but do not let the light travel straight through. Instead, the light is scattered into many different directions, so an object appears distorted or fuzzy through a translucent material. Frosted glass, tissue paper, and the waxed paper around the second sandwich are all examples of translucent materials.

Opaque materials do not let any light pass through them. Instead, they reflect light, absorb light, or both. When light enters a material but does not leave it, the light is absorbed. **Absorption** is the transfer of light energy to matter. Many materials, including wood, brick, and the brown paper around the third sandwich, are opaque.

3. Fill in the blanks to make the statements true.

   A. The sandwich wrapped in _____ is easy to see because the medium allows _____ of the light to pass through.

   B. The sandwich wrapped in _____ is obscured because the medium allows _____ of the light to pass through.

   C. The sandwich is completely blocked by the _____. That means the medium allows _____ of the light to pass through.

Matter Can Reflect Light

You can see an object only when light from that object enters your eyes. Some objects, such as a flame, give off, or emit, their own light. However, most objects do not emit light. We can see those objects because light from another source bounces off of them.

As you know, light waves travel from their source in all directions. If you could trace the path of one light wave, you would find that it travels in a straight line. When a light wave hits an object, the light wave may change direction. Mirrors and lenses are objects that change the path of light waves and affect the images that we see.

Ray Diagram

A ray diagram uses arrows, or rays, to show a path that light can take. The ray here changes direction because it hit a mirror.

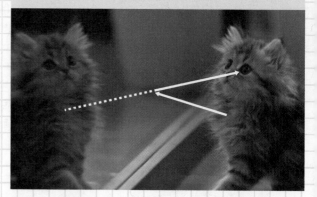

Mirrors

The bouncing of light off of a surface, such as a mirror, is called **reflection**. A mirror has a very smooth surface that reflects light. You might have used a mirror to get ready this morning. Because mirrors are very smooth, they reflect light in a uniform way that results in an image when the reflected light enters your eyes. Light can reflect from surface to surface before it enters your eyes. Light from a lamp, for example, might have reflected off your skin, then reflected off the mirror, and then entered your eyes. When you look at the mirror, you see yourself!

Do the Math
Practice Drawing Ray Diagrams

When you stand on one side of a one-way mirror, the glass appears to be transparent. You can see what is on the other side of the mirror. When you stand on the other side, the glass appears to be a mirror, so you see yourself.

4. **Draw** rays on the images below to illustrate the behavior of light for a one-way mirror.

Light Reflects in a Kaleidoscope

Kaleidoscopes have been entertaining people for about 200 years. A *kaleidoscope* is a toy that uses mirrors and little pieces of colored glass, bits of colored paper, or other small objects to produce beautiful, ever-changing patterns. The kaleidoscope below uses three mirrors set to form an equilateral triangle. Light enters one end of the tube, shines on the objects, and reflects off of the mirrors. Each mirror reflects the objects as well as the images of the objects in the other mirrors. Not only is there no end to the number of times each image is reflected, you'll also never see the same pattern twice!

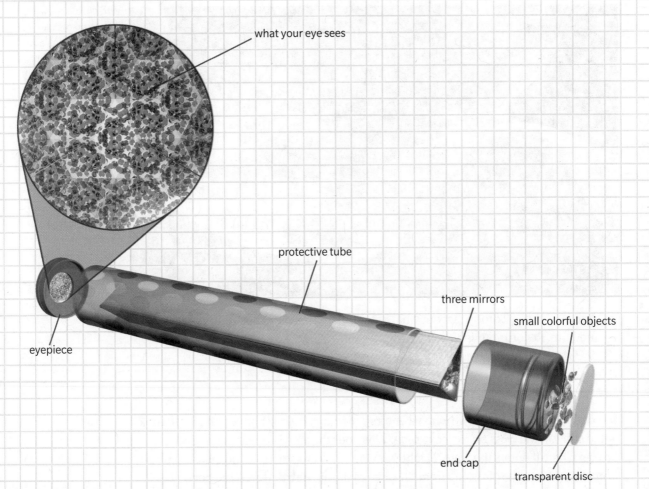

what your eye sees

protective tube

three mirrors

small colorful objects

eyepiece

end cap

transparent disc

5. In a kaleidoscope, light / matter enters the transparent / opaque part of the end cap. The end cap also houses the small colorful objects, which can be transparent, translucent, or opaque. Light interacts with these objects and is absorbed / reflected / refracted by the 60-degree angles of the mirrors. The result is a colorful honeycomb effect, which you can see through the eyepiece as light is absorbed by / is reflected off of / is refracted by the mirrors to your eye. Give the end cap a twist or shake, and the objects change position, producing yet a different pattern. The number of designs is infinite!

 EVIDENCE NOTEBOOK

6. Think about the ways that matter interacts with light. How do these interactions relate to the flashlight images at the beginning of the lesson? Record your evidence.

Matter Can Refract Light

Recall that light can travel through a vacuum or through a medium. When light of any wavelength travels through a vacuum, it always travels at the same speed. However, light travels slower in a medium. In fact, light of different wavelengths travel at different speeds in a medium. Shorter wavelengths are slowed more than longer wavelengths. Think about how a prism separates light into a spectrum. In a prism, the speed of shorter-wavelength violet light is less than the speed of longer-wavelength red light.

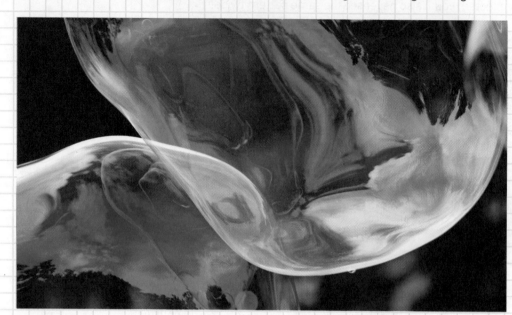

Why do we see a spectrum of color in bubbles? Think about one bubble. Light bends as it enters the bubble. The light is then reflected inside the bubble and bends again as it leaves the bubble. The different combinations of many light rays bending and reflecting create the beautiful colors.

7. **Act** With a small group, act out what can happen when light encounters a new medium. Record your idea below.

Not only does light slow down when it enters a medium, it also changes direction. Look at the straw in the glass on the next page. Why does the straw appear to be bent or broken where it enters the water? Light from the straw changes direction when it passes from the water to the glass and from the glass to the air. **Refraction** is the bending or change in direction of a light wave as it passes from one medium into another. This bending of a light wave is due to the change in speed of the wave as it enters a new medium.

8. When light enters the medium of a prism, light slows down / speeds up. The speed of each wavelength of color changes by a different amount. These changes in speed cause light to refract / reflect by different amounts, and that's why we see separate colors of light. Similarly, when light reflected from a straw travels from the water to the glass and then to the air, light slows down / speeds up. It changes speed each time it enters a new medium. These changes in speed cause light to refract / reflect, resulting in the appearance of a broken straw. Both examples show the bouncing / bending of light waves as a result of changes in wave speed / wavelength as the waves pass from one medium to another.

Hands-On Lab
Make a Penny Disappear

Observe how viewing an object through different media affects what you see.

MATERIALS
- beaker
- index card
- penny
- water

Procedure and Analysis

STEP 1 Place the penny on a flat surface like a lab table or a desk. Next, carefully set the beaker on top of the penny. Then place the index card on top of the beaker so that it covers the opening.

STEP 2 Look through the side of the container. Can you see the penny? _____

STEP 3 Tilt the index card and fill the beaker with water. Replace the index card.

STEP 4 Look through the side of the container. Can you see the penny? _____
Lift the index card and look again. Can you see the penny? _____

STEP 5 How did adding the water affect your observations? Why do you think this happened?

STEP 6 Draw ray diagrams to show how the path of light waves affected what you observed in Step 2 and Step 4.

Optical Illusions Caused by Refraction

Your mind can play tricks on you because of refraction. The straw in the picture and the coin in the activity are two examples of optical illusions caused by refraction. When you look at an object that is underwater, the light reflecting off the object does not travel in a straight line. The light refracts at an angle as it passes between the air and the water. Because our brains always interpret light as traveling in a straight line, the images that we perceive don't match. For example, the light reflected by the upper part of the straw does, indeed, travel in the air in a straight line to your eye. But the light from the lower part of the straw refracts as it passes from the water to the air. The refracted light then travels in a straight line to your eye. Your brain interprets these light rays as coming from different sources. This causes the illusion that the part of the straw in the water is disconnected from the part out of the water.

Refraction explains why the straw appears broken.

Convex Lenses

A lens is a clear optical tool that bends light. Lenses affect how we see images. The type of image depends on the shape of the lens and how close the object is to the lens. A convex lens is thicker at the center than at the edges. Think of parallel light waves pointing toward a lens and passing through it. If the lens is convex, then the waves *converge*, or move toward one another. Convex lenses form different kinds of images. You can see how two of these images are formed in the diagrams below. Convex lenses are used to magnify or focus light, so they are used in tools such as magnifying glasses, telescopes, and microscopes. Convex lenses may be used in eyeglasses to correct farsighted vision. *Farsightedness* happens when the eye is too short, which causes the lens to focus light behind the retina. A convex lens placed in front of a farsighted eye helps the lens in the eye focus the light on the retina.

Explore
ONLINE!

Convex Lenses Refract Light Waves to Create Images

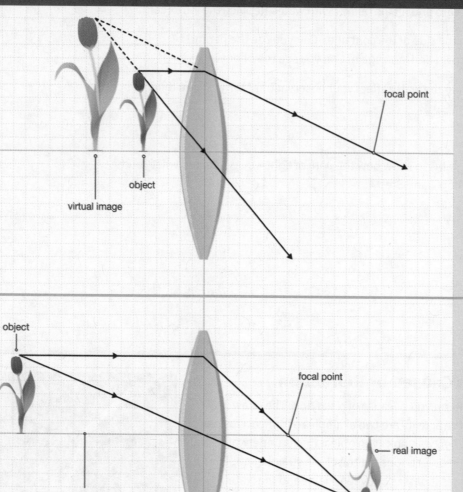

When light rays pass through a convex lens, the rays are refracted toward each other. An object that is close to the convex lens forms an image that is right-side up and larger than the object. Because light does not travel through this image, it is referred to as a *virtual image*. A virtual image cannot be projected.

An object that is far from a convex lens forms an image that is upside down and smaller. Because light does pass through this image, it is referred to as a *real image*. A real image can be projected onto a screen. Projectors, like the ones used to show movies, use convex lenses to project real images onto a movie screen.

9. **Discuss** Suppose you were looking at a leaf through a convex lens. With a partner, discuss what you might see if you put the lens very close to the leaf.

Concave Lenses

A concave lens is thinner at the center than at the edges. Think, again, of parallel light waves pointing toward a lens and passing through it. If the lens is concave, then the parallel light waves *diverge*, or move away from one another. You can see one way that a concave lens forms an image in the diagram below. Because the light rays entering a concave lens bend away from each other, the rays never meet. Concave lenses are used to spread light, often in combination with other lenses in telescopes and binoculars. Concave lenses are also used in microscopes and in eyeglasses to correct nearsighted vision. Nearsightedness occurs when the eye is too long, causing the lens to focus light in front of the retina. A nearsighted person can see something clearly only if it is nearby. A concave lens placed in front of a nearsighted eye refracts the light outward. The lens in the eye can then focus the light on the retina.

Concave Lenses Refract Light Waves to Create Images

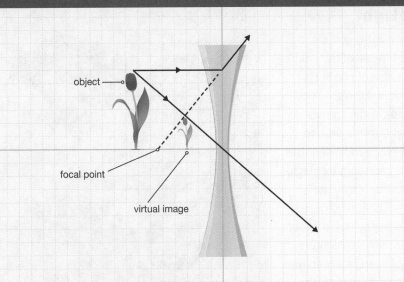

object

focal point

virtual image

When light rays pass through a concave lens, the rays are refracted away from each other. Concave lenses form virtual images that are smaller than the object. A concave lens cannot form a real image because light rays passing through a concave lens bend outward and never meet.

10. Apply what you have learned about lenses to predict what objects a person with nearsightedness can see clearly.

11. Think about a young bird learning to catch fish. Why might the bird not be successful at first?

Birds, such as seagulls, fly above the water and swoop down to grab fish with their beaks.

Matter Can Filter Light

Imagine that the strawberry and the broccoli floret in the top image of the diagram are sitting on your desk. In normal, unfiltered light, the strawberry appears mostly red and the broccoli appears mostly green. If you put a red filter over the light source, the strawberry would still appear mostly red, but the broccoli would appear mostly black. This is because you filtered out all colors except red. If you replace the red filter with a green filter, your perception will change again. The strawberry now appears mostly black while the broccoli appears mostly green. Only green light passes through the filter.

The Primary Colors of Light

If you were asked how to get white light, you'd probably answer, "you must combine all of the colors of light." That is true. But you can also get light that appears white by adding together just three colors of light—red, blue, and green. Look at the strawberry and the broccoli in the filtered light. If you were to place a blue filter in front of either the red filter or the green filter, both objects would appear mostly black. That is because these three colors absorb all the wavelengths of the other two. Red, blue, and green are referred to as the *primary colors of light*. No light will pass through two different primary color filters. However, these three colors of light can be combined in different ratios to produce many different colors.

12. **Draw** Would an orange still appear orange if you observed it through a blue filter? Create a diagram to show the effect of a blue filter on your perception of the color of an orange.

Light Color Affects Our Perception of Objects

Explore how filtered light that strikes an object affects the perceived color of the object.

Color Addition

When colors of light combine, you see different colors. Combining colors of light is called *color addition*. When two primary colors of light are added together, you see a *secondary color of light*. The secondary colors of light are cyan, magenta, and yellow. The diagram shows how the primary colors combine to form the secondary colors and white. The colors on most television, smartphone, and monitor screens are produced using color addition. The illuminated screen is made up of groups of tiny red, green, and blue dots. Each dot glows when hit by an electron beam. The colors given off by the glowing dots add together to produce all the different colors you see on the screen. Splatter a few tiny drops of water on a screen and look very closely. What do you see?

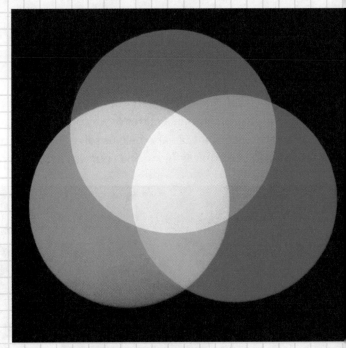

Primary colors of light combine to produce white light. Secondary colors of light are the result of two primary colors added together.

13. What color of light is produced when red light is added to green light?

    A. white

    B. cyan

    C. yellow

    D. blue

Engineer It

Engineering Solutions to Light Pollution

Nighttime lighting meets societal needs, but it also contributes to a condition known as *light pollution*. Light pollution is the term for excess nighttime lighting that obscures our view of the night sky, negatively affects wildlife, and wastes energy.

14. Draw Unshaded outdoor lights are one contributor to light pollution. Apply your knowledge of mirrors, lenses, and filters to design a shaded parking lot light that reduces excess nighttime light. Use ray diagrams to support your design.

Using Light to Solve Problems

As we've seen, the behavior of light helps us explain many common phenomena, such as why we see ourselves in a mirror or why objects appear as certain colors. Understanding the behavior of light can also help us solve real-world problems. For example, how could you apply your knowledge to find your way around dark corners or hallways?

It's difficult to illuminate a dark path when it bends around corners.

Have you ever seen a movie where the characters used polished mirrors to direct sunlight into a maze of darkened tombs and passageways? Does that really work? Is the light bright enough, even after it's reflected so many times? How do they direct the light exactly where they want it? Could you do something similar? Could you direct light through a maze?

15. Think about how you could design, build, and test a light maze. What specific behaviors of light will be essential to the success of your design? What specific behaviors of light might be obstacles to success? Record your ideas.

Hands-On Lab
Light Up a Maze

Think about all the ways that light behaves. For example, mirrors can reflect light, and lenses can refract light. Prisms can separate the colors of light by frequency, and filters can remove particular colors of light. You've seen how light behaves with each of these devices individually. Your challenge now is to apply your knowledge of the behaviors of light to solve a problem. Follow the steps of the engineering design process to solve your problem.

MATERIALS
- blue filter
- box, cardboard
- clay
- flashlight
- masking tape
- mirrors, small, flat
- protractor
- scissors
- tagboard/cardboard

Procedure and Analysis

STEP 1 Using what you know about the way light interacts with mirrors, plan and sketch a labeled diagram for your light maze design per the criteria below. Note the position of the mirrors and other items, as well as the opening, exit, and "treasure room." Then ask your teacher to check your plan.

Your maze must meet the following criteria:
- Light must enter through one opening and exit through another.
- Light must make at least three turns inside the maze.
- The maze must have three chambers. Designate one chamber as the treasure room.
- Light must be split into at least two beams.
- Light entering the treasure room must be blue.
- White light must illuminate a target.

The maze must meet the following constraint:
- Only materials provided by your teacher may be used.

STEP 2 Once your teacher has approved your plan, build a prototype of your maze, starting with the box. Poke starter holes with pencils and then carefully cut the holes out to allow light to enter and exit the maze. Label these openings "entrance" and "exit." Place the mirrors and other items in the box, using clay or tape and cardboard to position them properly. Also be sure to position the treasure room.

STEP 3 Test your prototype to make sure that it works as you intended. How will you check that the mirrors and other components are positioned correctly?

STEP 4 Evaluate the prototype light maze you constructed. Did you encounter any problems? If so, describe how you would modify your maze to eliminate those problems.

STEP 5 Why are the mirrors in the light maze important for solving the problem?

 Engineer It

Propose a Solution Using Sunlight

Tucked away in a valley surrounded by steep mountains is the small town of Rjukan in Norway. Because of its location, it gets sunlight only about six months out of the year. Not much! But the townspeople have a solution. On one of the mountains, they've installed three huge mirrors to direct sunlight to the town square below during the dark months.

16. What other ways could directed sunlight be used to solve a problem? Use examples in your explanation.

The sun mirrors of Rjukan illuminate an oval area of the town square where the townspeople can gather and enjoy a bit of sun.

_____

_____

_____

_____

_____

_____

17. Which statements do you think are true about the light in Rjukan?

A. Sunlight travels to the sun mirrors on the mountain and is reflected off of the mirrors to the town square below.

B. Light is reflected from the town square back up to the mirrors on the mountain.

C. Because the sun mirrors are very smooth and shiny, they reflect sunlight in a uniform way.

D. The sun mirrors could be replaced with sun lenses to reflect sunlight to the town square below.

Continue Your Exploration

Name: _____ Date: _____

Check out the path below or go online to choose one of the other paths shown.

| How Do Periscopes Work? | • **Hands-On Labs** 🖐
• **What Causes a Rainbow?**
• **Propose Your Own Path** | *Go online to choose one of these other paths.* |

Periscopes are devices that use mirrors and lenses to help people see around obstacles. Most people think of periscopes in submarines, where sailors can see above the water even while the submarine is still underwater. Periscopes, though, are also used to see over walls or around corners, to see out of parade floats and tanks, and to see inside pipes or machinery. Very simple periscopes can be constructed out of cardboard tubes and small mirrors. Let's see how light is reflected in a simple periscope.

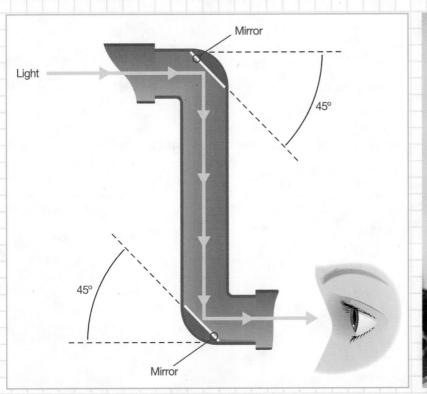

This periscope is engineered so that spectators at golf tournaments can see over the heads of people in the crowd.

Continue Your Exploration

1. Explain what you think would happen if you increased the length of a periscope.

In a plane mirror, the distance between the mirror and the object is the same as the distance between the mirror and the image. The image appears as if behind the mirror. This is true even if the image is of another image. This is what's happening when the image in the top mirror of the periscope is reflected in the bottom mirror of the periscope. The overall result is a smaller image that reaches the eye. Long periscopes like the ones used in submarines have magnifying lenses between the mirrors to enlarge the image.

2. How could you change the design of the periscope to let you see behind you?

3. Would this periscope be useful on a dark night? Use specific behaviors of light to support your argument.

4. **Collaborate** With a partner, discuss how a light wave travels in a periscope. Brainstorm how you could recycle everyday items to make a periscope, and then make a plan that you can share with the class.

Can You Explain It?

Name: _____   Date: _____

Revisit the photos that show how light behaves against three different surfaces.

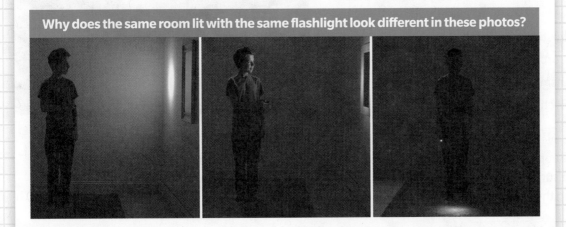

Why does the same room lit with the same flashlight look different in these photos?

 EVIDENCE NOTEBOOK

Refer to the notes in your Evidence Notebook to help you explain how the behavior of light affects what we see and how we see it.

1. State your claim. Make sure your claim explains how the same light source in the same room can produce such different results.

2. Summarize the evidence you have gathered to support your claim and explain your reasoning.

Checkpoints

Answer the following questions to check your understanding of the lesson.

Use the photo to answer Questions 3–5.

3. What behavior of light is being shown by the sphere?

   A. refraction

   B. absorption

   C. transmission

   D. reflection

4. Light travels in a *straight line / curved line*. However, the image on the sphere appears curved. Why? The sphere is a *lens / mirror*, so as light hits its curved surface, light *bounces off of / bends around* it at odd angles, causing the image to appear distorted.

5. What would happen if the sphere were painted solid black?

   A. The image on the sphere would be the same but darker.

   B. All of the light hitting the sphere would be absorbed by the sphere.

   C. The image on the sphere would no longer appear distorted.

   D. Some of the light hitting the sphere would be refracted by the sphere.

   E. The sphere would change from being transparent to opaque.

Use the photo to answer Question 6.

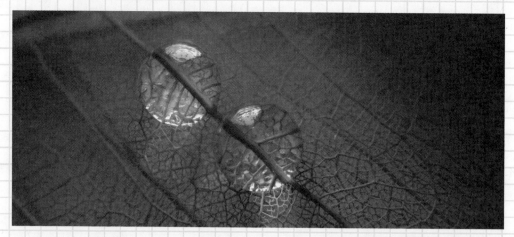

6. Because of *absorption / refraction / reflection*, the veins of the leaf are magnified where the droplets of water are. Light, which travels at a certain speed in air, travels through the water droplets at a different speed. Light slows down and *bends / bounces* as it moves from one medium to another. In fact, each water droplet acts as a *mirror / concave lens / convex lens*, causing the veins to appear larger.

Interactive Review

Complete this section to review the main concepts of the lesson.

Light can be transmitted through matter or can be absorbed by matter so that light enters it but does not leave it. Matter can also change the path that light takes.

A. How does light interact with each of the following types of matter: a transparent object, a mirror, a lens?

Understanding of the behavior of light can be applied to solve real-world problems. For example, devices can be designed and built to make use of the way light interacts with mirrors, lenses, prisms, and filters.

B. How can light be used to solve a problem? Give an example.

Choose one of the activities to explore how this unit connects to other topics.

☐ Music Connection

Sound Waves and Music Music is a mixture of sounds that have different pitches and volumes. Musical instruments are designed to produce a range of pitches. Musicians know how to play instruments to produce the pitch and volume of the sounds they need to make music.

Choose a musical instrument. Research how your instrument produces different pitches and volumes. Create a multimedia presentation to share with the class that explains how the instrument works. Include a simple mathematical model that shows how the properties of the sound waves relate to the frequency and volume.

☐ Social Studies Connection

Radar in World War II *Radar* stands for *ra*dio *d*etection *a*nd *r*anging. It uses electromagnetic waves to detect distant objects, such as airplanes or rainstorms. Great advances in radar were made during World War II in an effort to provide military forces with an advantage.

Research how radar was developed to solve a specific problem during the Second World War. Write a report that includes an explanation of the impact radar had on the war. Use reliable evidence to support your main points.

☐ Life Science Connection

Animal Senses Many animals see and hear the world differently than humans. They can detect sounds or electromagnetic waves that humans cannot detect. They use these senses to communicate and survive.

Research how animals can sense sound or electromagnetic waves that humans cannot sense. Choose one animal and write a screenplay for a nature television documentary that explains how the animal's senses differ from humans, how the animal's sensory organs allow it to sense waves, and how the animal uses its senses to communicate or survive.

Name: _____   Date: _____

Complete this review to check your understanding of the unit.

Use the photograph to answer Question 1.

1. The duck makes a wave in the water as it moves. Which statements describe the wave? Select all that apply.

   A. The wave is a mechanical wave.

   B. Water particles move away from the duck with the wave.

   C. The wave transfers energy through the water away from the duck.

   D. The amplitude of the wave decreases as the energy in the wave spreads out.

Use the diagram to answer Questions 2–3.

Sunlight

2. Which statements describe the waves of light that exit the droplet? Select all that apply.

   A. They travel at different speeds through space.

   B. They have different wavelengths from each other.

   C. They traveled at different speeds through the water droplet.

   D. They have a different frequency range than the light that entered the droplet.

3. Rainbows form because of the behaviors of visible sunlight in water droplets. Sunlight is refracted / reflected / absorbed when it enters a droplet. It is refracted / reflected / refracted and reflected on the opposite side of the droplet. Then it is refracted / reflected / emitted when it leaves the droplet.

---

4. A song with high and low frequencies is sung in a theater without a sound system. Which music notes will travel the farthest in the theater?

   A. The high frequency notes

   B. The low frequency notes

   C. High and low notes will travel equally far

   D. Neither will travel without a sound system

5. Fill in the blanks with green, yellow, or all other colors. In the fall, the leaves of an aspen tree change from green to yellow because the leaves reflect and absorb different wavelengths of light.

   The green leaves reflect _____ light and absorb _____.

   The yellow leaves reflect _____ light and absorb _____.

Name: _____   **Date:** _____

6. Complete the table by providing at least one example of how these wave behaviors relate to each big concept.

Wave Behaviors	Patterns	Structure and Function	Energy and Matter
Transmission			
Absorption			
Reflection			
Refraction			

Use the image to answer Questions 7–9.

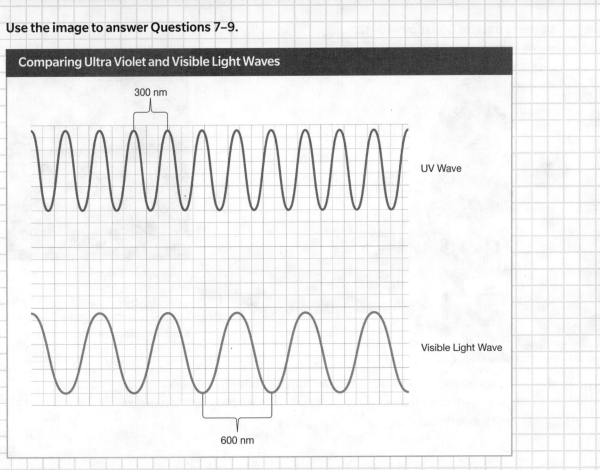

Comparing Ultra Violet and Visible Light Waves

300 nm

UV Wave

Visible Light Wave

600 nm

7. Compare the wavelength, frequency, and amplitude of the visible and ultraviolet light waves. Explain the relationship between wavelength and frequency.

8. Which wave transfers more energy in one minute? State your claim, provide evidence, and explain how your evidence supports your claim.

9. Using the wavelengths shown in the diagram, describe what will happen when ultraviolet light waves and visible light waves from the sun reach Earth's atmosphere. How does the behavior of the light waves relate to their frequency?

Use the images to answer Questions 10–12.

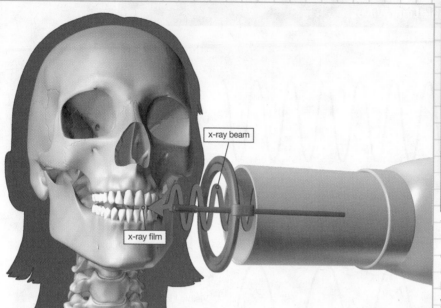

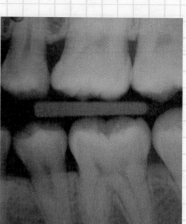

This diagram shows how an x-ray image of teeth is taken at the dentist's office. The lighter areas in the resulting x-ray image of the teeth are like the shadows that you see when you block visible light.

10. Based on the diagram and x-ray image, what can you conclude about how x-rays interact with your teeth and the tissues in your mouth? Use evidence of the behavior of light waves to support your claim.

11. Recall that sonograms are taken with sound waves. How is the process of taking sonograms different from the process of taking x-rays?

12. Sonograms, not x-rays, are used to take images of a developing fetus. Sound waves are also used to take images of the sea floor, while x-rays can provide information about the sun and distant bodies in space. How do the properties of sound waves and x-rays affect the ways they are used? Make a claim and use evidence to support it.

UNIT 1 PERFORMANCE TASK

Date:

Will your audience be able to hear you?

You are planning the production of a play. The play is going to be performed outdoors without microphones. There will be 100 tickets for each performance and the audience will sit on the ground or folding chairs. You need to design the seating area so that everyone in the audience will be able to hear the performers. Develop a proposal for a performance area that will maximize the audience's ability to hear the play.

The steps below will help guide your research and develop your recommendation.

Engineer It

1. **Define the Problem** Write a statement to clearly define the problem you are trying to solve. Identify the criteria and constraints that you need to consider in your design.

Unit 1 Waves   **85**

Engineer It

2. **Conduct Research** How will distance affect the audience's ability to hear sound? Research theaters without sound systems. How do these theaters use sound wave properties to ensure that all of the actors are heard?

3. **Develop a Model** Are there different types of seating arrangements that might work better than others? Apply your research to make a diagram or model of your seating area. Include how you expect the volume to change for audience members.

4. **Optimize a Solution** Compare your solution to the Royal Albert Hall in London, the Epidaurus Ancient Theatre in Greece, or the Vienna Musikverein in Vienna. How is your theater design different or similar? Based on what you know about sound, how is your solution more or less effective? Is your design the optimal solution? If not, modify your solution.

5. **Communicate** Present your design proposal to the class. Include design specifics such as seating arrangement and stage location. Explain why your design is the optimal solution. Ensure your presentation includes a thorough explanation of the properties of the sound wave behavior involved.

✓ **Self-Check**

	I identified the criteria and constraints of the problem.
	I described how sound volume changes with distance.
	I drew a diagram to model the seating arrangement that included how sounds would change.
	I provided a thorough explanation of my design proposal in a class presentation.

Information Transfer

Lesson 1 Communication and Waves 90

Lesson 2 Analog and Digital Signals 106

Lesson 3 Communication Technology 124

Unit Review 145

Unit Performance Task 149

How can we communicate with astronauts if sound waves cannot travel in space? Scientists and engineers work together to develop information transfer technology.

There are 30 seconds left in the final game of the World Cup. Your favorite player draws back his foot to attempt the game winning shot and . . . suddenly your screen goes blank from a power outage caused by a storm. Luckily, your family owns a battery-operated radio! You tune in just in time to hear: "GOAL!" Technologies we use every day send and receive information using wave energy. However, each technology has both advantages and limitations. In this unit, you will learn how scientists and engineers work together to handle information transfer challenges.

Why It Matters

Here are some questions to consider as you work through the unit. Can you answer any of the questions now? Revisit these questions at the end of the unit to apply what you discover.

Questions	Notes
What are different ways you receive information each day?	
A mailed letter is made out of paper and ink. What is an email or text message made out of?	
How do waves get "sent"? How are they "received"? What might get in their way?	
How has wireless information technology changed society? Where will it take us in the future?	
What challenges do engineers face when designing systems to send and receive wave information? What science concepts do they need to know to meet those challenges?	

Unit Starter: Predicting the Path of Light

Review reflection and refraction of light as you learn about how the reflecting telescope magnifies distant objects. This telescope captures information from a celestial object using a series of mirrors and lenses to bend light to our eye.

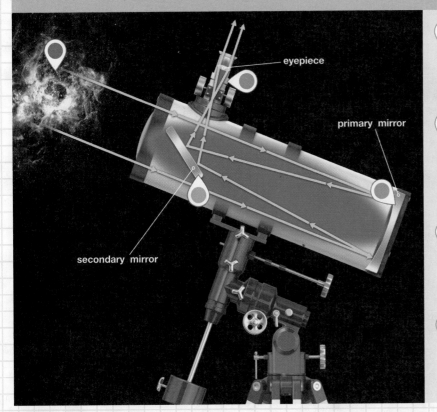

Light from the stars reflects off cosmic dust and travels long distances to reach the telescope. The light rays entering the telescope are roughly parallel.

The primary mirror captures the dim light coming from space far better than our eye. The curve of the mirror converges the light rays into an image small enough to focus onto the retina.

The secondary plane mirror does not cause the light rays to converge further. It simply redirects the light into the eyepiece.

The light is transmitted through the lens in the eyepiece. Because the surface of the lens is curved, the light will bend as it travels through, magnifying the image.

1. A telescope transfers information about a distant object to the observer, gathering more detail than the eye could alone. What properties of light allow the telescope to perform this function? Select all that apply.

   A. Light travels faster than sound.

   B. Light bounces off smooth surfaces at predictable angles.

   C. Light is comprised of electromagnetic waves.

   D. Light changes speed when entering a new substance.

Go online to download the Unit Project Worksheet to help you plan your project.

Unit Project

Emergency Broadcasting

How do local authorities get the word out quickly and clearly to emergency personnel, radio and TV stations, and area hospitals during a natural disaster? As part of a team of engineers, propose a plan for your city's emergency alert system.

Communication and Waves

Electromagnetic waves, transmitted between towers such as these, are used to communicate.

By the end of this lesson . . .

you will be able to explain why waves are used in today's communication technology.

CAN YOU EXPLAIN IT?

How can a spacecraft send messages across the Solar System?

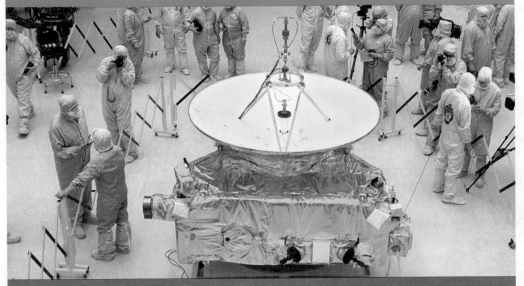

A spacecraft called New Horizons was launched from Earth on January 19, 2006. Its destination was Pluto, an icy dwarf planet. New Horizons reached Pluto nearly ten years later, on July 14, 2015. After traveling more than 4 billion kilometers, it was still able to communicate with Earth.

1. Spacecraft like New Horizons can travel great distances from Earth. And yet we are still able to communicate with these spacecraft! What might make this long-distance communication possible?

 EVIDENCE NOTEBOOK As you explore the lesson, gather evidence to help explain how a spacecraft could send messages across the Solar System.

Exploring Long-Distance Communication

Think of the ways in which you interact with your friends and family every day. When you are together, you might speak, gesture, or use sign language to share ideas and experiences. These are examples of *communication,* or the sharing of information between people. If you are right next to a friend, it is easy to carry on a conversation. If you and your friend are farther away, it is harder to see or hear each other. If you are too far from each other, communication is impossible without the help of technology.

When two people are close together, they can easily communicate by speaking or gesturing.

2. What do you think are the key features of a communication device?

As they move farther apart, they may have difficulty seeing or hearing one another.

3. Make a list of communication devices. Which of these devices do you think is the most useful? Explain your answer.

People who are very far apart cannot directly communicate at all unless they use technology. Modern communication devices such as cell phones are able to quickly send images, sound, and other information over great distances.

Signals

Tools that allow people to communicate at a distance have existed for thousands of years. Early forms of long-distance communication included the use of drum patterns and controlled fires. The sounds made by a drum and the light from a fire or a lamp are examples of signals. A **signal** is anything that can transmit information.

4. What do the historical communication technologies in these photos have in common?

Drums have often been used to communicate across long distances. Drums can produce loud sound signals that can be heard from far away.

The light from lamps and lanterns has also been used as a signal. A lantern allows for more control than a signal fire and can be used to send more complex light signals.

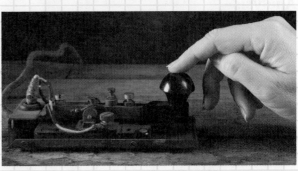

Samuel Morse invented an electric telegraph in 1837. The telegraph sent electric signals through a wire. The telegraph could quickly send complex messages over a long distance.

Encode and Decode Information

Communication technologies all involve sending information. But communication only happens when information is received and understood by another person. A sequence of drumbeats may carry a specific meaning for one person, but not another. When the sender and receiver of a signal agree on what the signal means, they have encoded information into the signal. Information is represented in a signal by **encoding.** Without encoding, no communication would be possible. A warning message sent by a fire is only helpful if the people who see it understand how to interpret, or *decode*, the message. If two people do not agree on what a signal means, they cannot communicate effectively.

Hands-On Lab
Encode a Message

You will design a way to encode a message. You and a partner will create an encoding system and use it to encode and decode a message.

Many types of signals require putting information in a different form. For example, a drum cannot send pictures. A written letter cannot send a sound. People using methods of long-distance communication have to find ways to encode many types of information into a signal. In order to transmit information, it often has to be put in another form.

Procedure

STEP 1 Create a visual code that allows you to encode a short message. Write a key on one index card that would allow your partner to decode a message written in your code.

STEP 2 Write a short message using your encoding system on a second index card.

STEP 3 Give both cards to your partner and allow him or her to decode the message.

STEP 4 Trade roles with your partner. Repeat Steps 1–3.

Analysis

STEP 5 **Discuss** With your partner, discuss the following questions: Was it easier to encode a message or decode a message? Did anything about this process surprise you? How could you revise your code to make it easier to encode and decode messages? Record your answers.

EVIDENCE NOTEBOOK

5. Does the New Horizons probe need to encode the information that it sends? Consider how the information it gathers might be sent back to Earth and interpreted. Record your evidence.

6. Morse code uses combinations of two pulses of different lengths to represent numbers and letters. A dash (—) is used to represent a long pulse, and a dot (•) is used to represent a short pulse. When messages are sent, the dashes and dots are turned into sounds. Each dash is a long beep and each dot is a short beep. A combination of dashes and dots can be used to represent each letter in the alphabet. Using the International Morse Code key shown, decode this three letter message: • • • — — — • • •

A •—	N —•	1 •————
B —•••	O ———	2 ••———
C —•—•	P •——•	3 •••——
D —••	Q ——•—	4 ••••—
E •	R •—•	5 •••••
F ••—•	S •••	6 —••••
G ——•	T —	7 ——•••
H ••••	U ••—	8 ———••
I ••	V •••—	9 ————•
J •———	W •——	0 —————
K —•—	X —••—	
L •—••	Y —•——	
M ——	Z ——••	

7. **Collaborate** With a partner, try the following activity. Send a message to your partner using Morse code. You can hum short and long sounds to represent dots and dashes. For example, to send the letter "C" you would say, "daaah dih daaah dih." Try decoding your partner's message and then switch roles. Record any difficulties that you encountered when sending Morse code messages to one another.

Make Encoding and Decoding Easier

Most communication devices that you use, such as a computer or a cell phone, rely on encoded signals to send information. Fortunately, you do not have to manually translate a message into electrical pulses each time you use a computer. You do not have to decode the incoming signal either. That would take a very long time! Most of today's communication technologies encode and decode information automatically.

Analyze Communication Methods

8. Consider the examples of communication technologies described so far. Which of these technologies requires the sender to encode a message before sending it?

_____

_____

_____

_____

Analyzing Waves in Communication

Nearly every form of communication is made possible by waves. *Waves* are disturbances that transfer energy from one place to another. Waves are well suited for sending information because they do not permanently move matter, and they can be varied in many ways to hold information. One common type of wave is sound, which we use to talk to each other. However, sound, like all waves, loses energy as it travels. Different types of waves lose energy at different rates. You might be able to see a light from many miles away at night, but you could not hear your friend singing from the same distance.

Explore
ONLINE!

Lighthouses indicate the location of land to ships at sea. While they have been mostly replaced by radar, some lighthouses are still used today.

9. What type of wave is used by this lighthouse to signal ships? What might be some advantages of using this type of wave to communicate?

10. **Language SmArts** Recall some of the communication methods that you have considered. Choose a long-distance communication method, and explain how it uses waves to send encoded information. Use diagrams to clarify your explanation.

Twentieth-Century Communication Technology

In the twentieth century, communication technology started to focus on transmitting information over longer distances. Signals such as sound waves cannot travel over extreme distances. To solve this problem, the technologies that were developed in the last century began using radio waves and electric signals to transmit information over long distances.

Radios send and receive information wirelessly using radio waves, a type of electromagnetic wave. By the 1920s, radios were able to encode and decode information, allowing audio information to be sent over radio waves.

Telephones send and receive audio information. The first phones encoded sound as an electric signal that was sent through a wire. Many phones are now wireless and send information encoded as electromagnetic waves.

11. What features did twentieth-century radios, telephones, and televisions share?

Televisions receive audio and video information. The first home televisions became popular in the 1940s. Televisions are able to receive information from radio waves and from electric signals that are sent through cables.

Electromagnetic Waves and Electric Signals

Over time, engineers have started to make communication devices that use electromagnetic waves and electric signals. Electric signals are able to carry information over extreme distances through wires, using changing electric signals that behave like waves. Electromagnetic waves can travel long distances and be sent through the atmosphere into space. We now use devices such as cell phones and computers that rely on electromagnetic waves to communicate over long distances.

EVIDENCE NOTEBOOK

12. What type of signal might the New Horizons probe use? What type of signal can travel through space? Record your evidence.

Advantages of Electromagnetic Waves

Electromagnetic waves, such as radio waves, have several characteristics that make them ideal to use as signals. Electromagnetic waves can be modified to contain information. By precisely varying certain properties of an electromagnetic wave, communication devices can encode images, videos, sound, and other types of information into the wave. Electromagnetic waves also travel at a high speed of about 300,000 km/s. This speed allows for very fast communication over long distances.

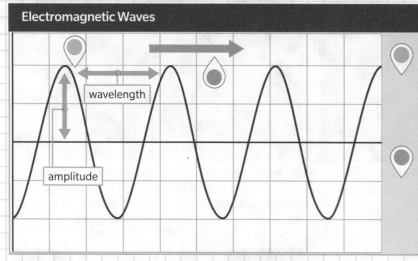

Electromagnetic Waves

wavelength

amplitude

Wave Properties Communication devices can encode information into an electromagnetic wave by changing a property of a wave, such as the wave's amplitude or wavelength.

Speed All electromagnetic waves travel at the same high, constant speed. Changing the amplitude or frequency of an electromagnetic wave does not affect its speed.

13. Which properties of radio waves make them useful for sending information?

Engineer It

Compare Communication Methods

Imagine that you are exploring a forest with some friends. You all realize that you need to be able to signal one another if one of you gets lost. Each person in your group has a cellphone, a whistle, and a flashlight. Consider the features of each device and how useful the device would be as an emergency signal.

14. What are the advantages and disadvantages of each communication device?

_____

_____

_____

_____

_____

_____

_____

Investigating How Waves Are Modified

Many communication technologies use waves that carry encoded information. But how are encoded messages incorporated into these waves? The answer to this question has to do with the properties of the waves.

15. Do any of these waves seem like they might be carrying information? Explain your answer.

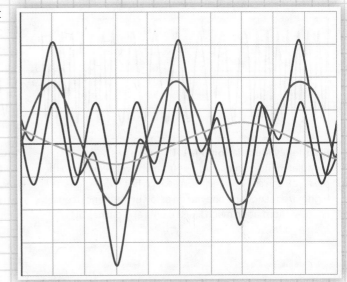

Wave Modulation

When information has been encoded into an electromagnetic wave, we say that the wave has been modulated. *Modulation* is the process of varying a property of a wave in order to encode information into the wave. Usually the amplitude or the frequency of the wave is varied so that complex information can be communicated.

Modulated Wave

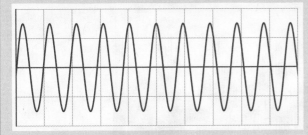

This wave has not been modulated. No information has been encoded into the wave.

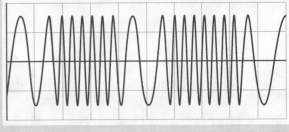

This wave has been modulated. Information has been encoded into the wave.

 16. Do the Math What property of the modulated wave has been modified?

Explore ONLINE!

17. How has that property been changed in this signal?

Types of Modulation

There are several different ways to modulate a wave. One or more properties of a wave can be varied to encode information. Two of the most common wave properties that are modulated are the amplitude and frequency. You may have noticed that radios often have an AM/FM button. Most modern radios are able to decode waves that have had their amplitude modulated (AM) or have had their frequency modulated (FM).

Frequency and Amplitude Modulation

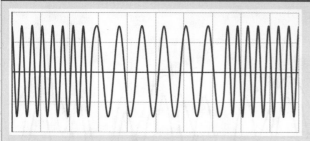

Frequency Modulation (FM) This wave has been modulated. Its frequency varies from one wavelength to the next. You can see how this wave, which has two regions of higher frequency and one region of lower frequency, could encode information much like the dots and dashes of Morse code.

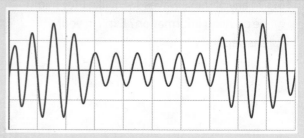

Amplitude Modulation (AM) This wave has been modulated. The amplitude of this wave has been changed. Frequency modulation and amplitude modulation are two different encoding methods. Encoding the same information using these two methods will result in waves that have different shapes.

Engineer It
Explain Recorded Audio

The music that you listen to on a computer is a sound that was recorded far away from you and possibly long ago. It is a form of long-distance communication. Many computer programs are able to display a music file as a wave. Look at the signal pictured and consider what type of modulation is being used to store information in the wave.

18. Has the frequency or amplitude of the wave in the image been modified? Explain your answer.

_____

_____

_____

_____

Continue Your Exploration

Name: _____   Date: _____

Check out the path below or go online to choose one of the other paths shown.

AM and FM Radio Waves

- **Hands-On Labs** 🖐
- **Communication Devices**
- **Propose Your Own Path**

Go online to choose one of these other paths.

When you use a radio, you are able to select individual channels for different radio stations. Each station is a range of radio frequencies. When you tune to a station, your radio picks up radio waves in that frequency range. Radio stations modulate radio waves in their assigned frequency range to transmit sound information.

1. In the United States, each FM radio station has a range of frequencies that is hundreds of times larger than the range of an AM radio channel. Why might this be? Consider the differences between FM and AM radio waves.

Continue Your Exploration

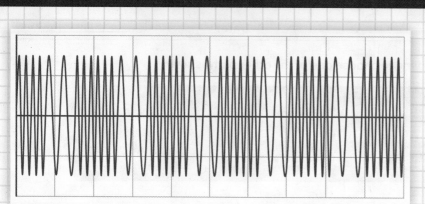

FM radio waves can transmit more information than AM radio waves.

2. The wider the frequency range that a radio station is given, the more information it can transmit. With their wider frequency ranges, FM radio channels are often used to transmit music, which requires high-quality sound. AM radio channels are often used to transmit talk radio, which has lower-quality sound requirements. How might the sound quality be affected if AM radio waves were used to transmit music?

   A. The music would have a lower-quality sound.

   B. The music would have a higher-quality sound.

   C. The music would sound the same as it would if transmitted using FM radio waves.

3. Radio waves with lower frequencies are able to travel much farther than radio waves with high frequencies can travel. In the United States, AM radio channels have lower frequencies than FM radio channels. What might be some uses of transmitting information longer distances using AM radio waves? Explain your answer.

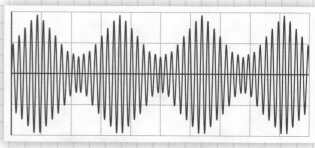

AM radio waves can be transmitted over much farther distances than FM radio waves.

4. **Collaborate** With a partner, devise a method for sending a Morse code message as an AM radio signal. Describe your method.

Can You Explain It?

Name: _____   Date: _____

Think about the New Horizons spacecraft and consider how information could be transmitted across billions of kilometers.

How can a spacecraft send messages across the Solar System?

 EVIDENCE NOTEBOOK

Refer to the notes in your Evidence Notebook to help you construct an explanation for how a spacecraft can send messages across the Solar System.

1. State your claim. Make sure your claim fully explains how a spacecraft can send messages over such a long distance.

2. Summarize the evidence you have gathered to support your claim and explain your reasoning.

Checkpoints

Answer the following questions to check your understanding of the lesson.

Use the diagram to answer Question 3.

3. What does changing the frequency do to the speed of this radio wave?

    A. It increases its speed.

    B. It decreases its speed.

    C. It does not affect the speed.

4. A radio tower transmits music to nearby radios. The radio tower uses radio waves, a type of electromagnetic wave, to transmit the music. Which statements accurately describe this situation? Choose all that apply.

    A. The radio tower encodes information into the radio wave signal.

    B. A listener will need a radio to decode the signal and listen to music.

    C. Information is encoded into the radio wave by modulating the radio wave.

Use the diagram to answer Questions 5.

5. This graph shows the amplitude of a wave changing / staying constant. The pattern of the amplitude would indicate that the wave is / is not modulated.

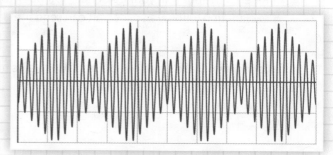

6. A CD can be encoded with music and vocal recordings. A CD player reads the information on the CD and translates it into sound waves. Which would be the best way to transmit the information on a CD the greatest distance?

    A. turning the volume all the way up on the CD player

    B. transmitting the information as a radio wave instead of a sound wave

    C. modifying the CD player to change the frequency of the sound waves

Interactive Review

Complete this section to review the main concepts of the lesson.

Many systems and technologies have been designed to communicate over long distances. They all send information that has been encoded into a signal.

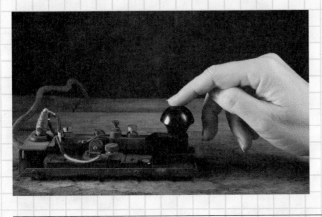

A. What must a receiver be able to do to understand a signal that is being sent to them?

Electromagnetic waves can move quickly and be encoded with information, making them ideal signals.

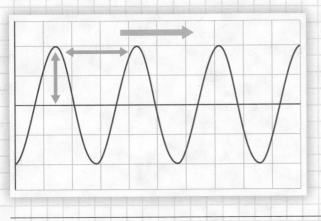

B. What are two methods that you could use to communicate with a friend? Describe two methods that each use a different type of signal.

Waves can be modulated in order to add information to the wave. Amplitude and frequency are properties of a wave that are commonly modulated.

C. Explain the relationship between modulating a wave and encoding information.

Analog and Digital Signals

Digital signals allow supercomputers and servers like these to quickly process large amounts of information.

By the end of this lesson . . .

you will be able to evaluate analog and digital signals to determine the strengths and weaknesses of each.

Go *online* to view the digital version of the Hands-On Lab for this lesson and to download additional lab resources.

CAN YOU EXPLAIN IT?

How can a video from the Internet appear the same every time you watch it?

Videos are shared on the Internet constantly. Some videos are watched billions of times from many different computers. Even though a video may have already been watched millions of times and is streaming from a server thousands of miles away, the video will still appear the same every time that you watch it.

Explore ONLINE!

1. What are some reliable ways to communicate across long distances? What do these methods have in common with the way a video is using the Internet?

EVIDENCE NOTEBOOK As you explore the lesson, gather evidence to help explain how an Internet video can appear the same every time you watch it.

Analyzing Analog and Digital Information

Not all information is the same. Some information exists as distinct values, such as the letters in a word. And some information can vary continuously, such as the sounds produced when you say a word out loud.

The thermometer on the left displays a digital signal. The thermometer on the right displays an analog signal.

Digital

Analog

2. How many values can the digital thermometer show between 25.0° and 25.4°? What are those values?

3. How many values can the analog thermometer show between 25.0° and 25.4°? Explain your answer.

Types of Information

Information can be either analog or digital. Digital information is not continuous. Instead, digital information consists of distinct values. The digital thermometer cannot show a temperature in between 25.0° and 25.1°. It is limited to showing a set number of values. Analog information is continuous. The analog thermometer can show smooth changes in temperature. There are marks that indicate specific temperatures, but the fluid level can be at any level between those marks as well.

4. What are some types of analog information?

If the amount of water in this cup were measured over time, the resulting data would be a set of continuous information.

Analog Information

Much of the information we deal with is analog information. For instance, your height is a piece of analog information. For convenience, we typically measure ourselves in feet and inches, but your height is not limited to those values. When you grow, you do not suddenly become one inch taller. Instead, you will slowly grow taller over time. If you grow from 5 feet tall to 5 feet and 1 inch tall, you will at some point have been every height in between those two measurements.

5. What are some types of digital information?

If the amount of soybeans in this bowl were measured over time, the resulting data would be a set of distinct values.

Digital Information

Digital information only exists as a series of values. For instance, if you were counting the number of students in your class, you would never have half a student. If you add a student to your class, you would not at any point have had a third of a student in your class. Instead, your class would suddenly just have one more student. The number of students in your class during a school year can only be certain numbers. That makes it a set of digital information.

Graph Analog and Digital Signals

Analog information and digital information have to be communicated in different ways. Whether information is communicated using a graph, a wave, or any other type of signal, the two types of information will be encoded differently. A signal containing analog information must be able to show all of the continuous information. A signal containing digital information must be able to clearly show the different distinct values.

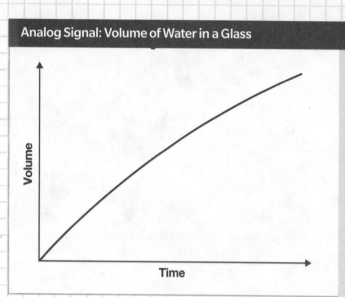

Analog Signal: Volume of Water in a Glass

This graph represents the volume of water in a cup as the water is being poured into the cup.

6. This graph contains analog information. What features of the graph indicate that it contains analog information?

Analog Signals

An **analog signal** is a signal that contains analog information. Analog information is continuous and can be any value. So, any signal that communicates analog information also must be continuous. A graph of analog information will show smooth changes in between values. The pictured graph shows how the volume of water increases smoothly, with no breaks in the graph. Every single part of the line communicates some information. The line does not simply jump between data points. Instead, it moves through a range of values. A light signal, a sound signal, or an electromagnetic wave signal could all be analog signals if analog information were encoded into them.

7. What do you notice about this graph compared
   to the graph of analog information?

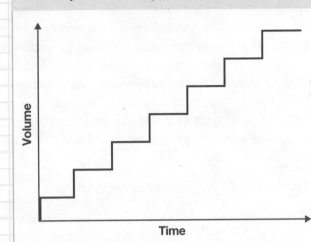

Digital Signal: Volume of Beans in a Bowl

This graph represents the volume of soybeans in a bowl
as the soybeans are being poured into the bowl.

Digital Signals

A **digital signal** is a signal that contains digital
information. Digital information is not continuous
and instead only contains a number of distinct
values. So, any signal that communicates digital
information will also be discontinuous. The pictured graph shows the volume increasing
as soon as a single soybean falls in. The graph moves between levels instead of varying
continuously. Other digital signals also follow this pattern of varying between levels.
For instance, the presence or lack of a signal fire can be a digital signal. When the fire is
present, people know that help is needed. When the fire is not present, everyone is safe.

Do the Math
Number of Levels in a Signal

8. These digital waves use different y-axis values to encode information. Write the
   number of different values shown in each graph.

Digital Wave A	Digital Wave B	Digital Wave C

_____   _____   _____

9. It might seem that a digital signal would need many levels to contain complex
   information. How might this requirement be avoided? Consider how we represent
   large numbers.

Binary Digital Signals

Computers were designed to make use of digital information that has only two different values. A computer processor consists of many switches that have two states—on and off. To communicate, computers use digital signals with two levels. These signals are known as binary signals. The two levels of the binary signal correspond to either an "on" or an "off" to a computer. To make binary signals easier to read, they are usually represented by a series of the numbers 1 and 0, which represent the values "on" and "off." In order to communicate complex information, long series of these 1s and 0s are strung together. Every piece of information that you see on a computer can be represented as a series of 1s and 0s.

Numbers in Binary	
Number	**Binary Code**
0	0
1	1
2	10
3	11
4	100
5	101
6	110
7	111
8	1000
9	1001

10. How might you graph a binary digital signal?

EVIDENCE NOTEBOOK

11. If you are streaming a video from a website, what type of signal is being sent to your computer from the website? Record your evidence.

Identify Signal Types

12. The word bank lists different types of signals that can be used to send a message or data. Put each item from the word bank in the table depending on which type of information the signal type is likely to send.

WORD BANK
- Signal fires
- Morse code
- Speech

Analog	Digital

Encoding Information in Waves

Both analog and digital information have to be encoded into a signal in order to be transmitted. Many communication devices, such as radios and cell phones, use electromagnetic waves as signals. Like other signals, electromagnetic waves are varied in different ways depending on the type of information that is being encoded into the signal. Recall that modulation is changing a property of a wave, such as its amplitude or wavelength, in order to encode information into the wave. The original electromagnetic wave, which is known as a *carrier wave*, is modulated. The carrier wave is modulated differently depending on the type of information that is being added to the wave.

13. How might you be able to tell if a modulated wave contains digital information instead of analog information?

Encoding Analog Signals

When analog information is encoded into an electromagnetic wave, the carrier wave is modulated continuously. In the pictured graphs, the amplitude of the wave is being modulated. The final modulated analog signal resembles the original carrier wave. However, the amplitude has been changed to encode the analog signal graph into the wave.

When analog information is added to a signal, the signal must be able to vary continuously. In this case, the amplitude of the modulated wave can be any value. The amplitude changes continuously instead of abruptly jumping between specific levels.

 14. Language SmArts How you can tell that this modulated signal contains analog information instead of digital information. Support your answer with evidence from the graph.

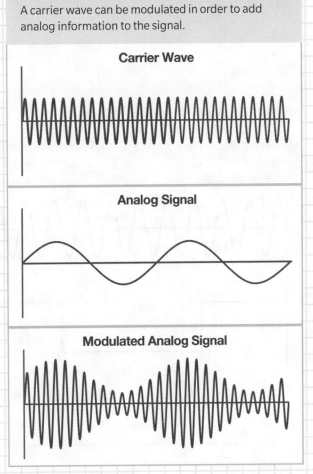

Encoding Analog Information

A carrier wave can be modulated in order to add analog information to the signal.

Carrier Wave

Analog Signal

Modulated Analog Signal

Encoding Digital Signals

An electromagnetic wave is modulated differently when digital information is encoded into the wave. In the pictured graphs, the amplitude of the wave is being modulated to represent two different values. The final modulated digital signal resembles the original carrier wave. However, the amplitude varies between two distinct levels. These two levels represent the two levels of the digital signal graph. When digital information is added to a wave, the wave does not vary continuously. Instead, it resembles a series of pulses.

15. Compare the final modulated digital signal to the modulated analog signal in the previous graph. How are they similar and how are they different?

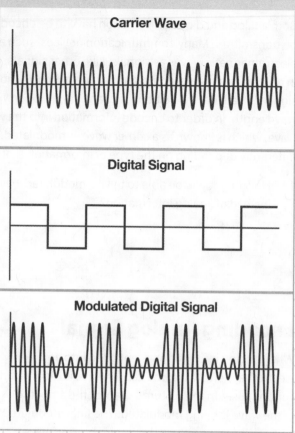

Encoding Digital Information

A carrier wave can be modulated in order to add digital information to the signal.

Carrier Wave

Digital Signal

Modulated Digital Signal

Modulate a Radio Wave

16. Using the carrier wave and digital signal provided, draw the modulated wave that would result.

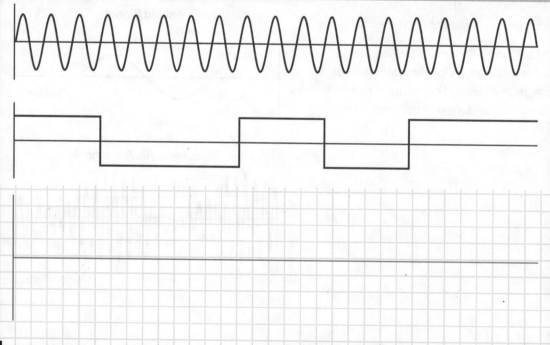

Explaining How Noise Affects Signals

When you talk to friends in a loud, busy room, it can be hard to understand what they are saying. Their voices might get drowned out by other sounds. You might hear someone else say something and think it was one of your friends. Your friends might need to speak loudly for you to understand them. The noise in the room makes it harder for you to understand what your friends are saying, because you are hearing other sounds at the same time.

17. Imagine you are in a room with a lot of noise and are trying to tell something to a friend. What are some ways that you could improve the communication between you and your friend?

18. Could a similar phenomenon occur when using signals such as signal fires or radio waves to communicate? Explain your answer.

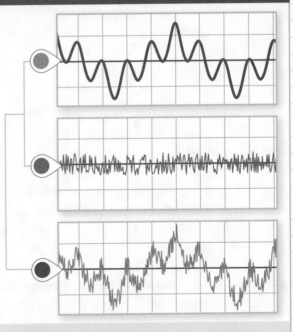

Noise in a Signal

Noise

The concept of noise does not only apply to sound. **Noise** is any unwanted change to a signal. When you hear a lot of other sounds in addition to your friends talking, the signals reaching you are different from the signals that your friends are sending. Sound from other activities is interfering with the sound of your friends' voices.

Noise can affect all types of signals. Sunlight can make it hard to see a fire. Electronics can interfere with electric signals. Noise can occur anytime a signal is transmitted, stored, or recorded. Whenever the signal that reaches the intended receiver is different from the signal that was originally transmitted, noise has affected the signal.

This analog wave represents a signal that is being transmitted.

This wave represents noise from inside the communication equipment or from the environment. The random spikes are formed by the combination of many unwanted waves that form noise.

This wave represents the original signal after noise has affected it. The signal is still similar, but now has random variations in it.

Hands-On Lab

Transmit and Record a Signal

You will be examining the noise that accumulates in analog and digital signals as they are sent and received.

Procedure and Analysis

STEP 1 Record yourself reading a sentence from a book.

STEP 2 Play the message back and record the message onto the second recording device. Do not make the second recording by connecting the two devices together with a cable. Instead, play the first recording, and make the second recording using the microphone of the other recording device.

STEP 3 Compare your two recordings.

STEP 4 What do you think might happen if you kept rerecording each new recording? Make a prediction and then test it.

STEP 5 Your original message was an analog signal. It was a recording of a continuous sound wave. Now record a digital signal and then repeat Steps 2–4. Remember that a digital signal needs two or more distinct levels.

STEP 6 Compare the results for your analog signal and your digital signal. How did your rerecordings compare to your initial recordings?

Noise in Analog Signals

Because the information in analog signals varies continuously, any noise that changes the wave becomes a part of the signal. Once noise has been added to an analog signal, there is no way to completely remove it. In the final version of the message that you recorded, it is impossible to tell what parts of the signal are noise and what parts are the original signal. When an analog signal is changed due to noise, the information in the signal is also changed.

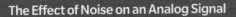

The Effect of Noise on an Analog Signal	
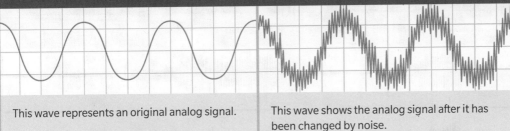	
This wave represents an original analog signal.	This wave shows the analog signal after it has been changed by noise.

Noise in Digital Signals

The information in digital signals is not continuous. Because the signal has defined levels, noise does not have as large an effect on the decoding of the signal. Think about the recordings you made of a digital signal. If the levels were recognizable enough, it was easy to tell the original signal from the noise. For instance, imagine that you recorded a signal that varied in between silence and a loud clap. When there is a loud clap, you can still hear it even if there is noise. Noise would not make the silent portions loud enough to be confused with claps. A digital signal can be designed to minimize the effect of noise. Unless there is so much noise that the different levels of the digital signal cannot be told apart, the information in a digital signal can be decoded reliably.

The Effect of Noise on a Digital Signal	
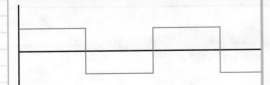	
This graph represents an original digital signal.	This wave shows the digital signal after it has been changed by noise. The different levels in a digital signal help to minimize the effect of noise.

EVIDENCE NOTEBOOK

19. When you are watching a video on the Internet, could there be any sources of noise that would make it hard to recognize the original signal? Record your evidence.

Explain Reliability in Signal Storage

Many methods have been used to store signals. Vinyl records are a method of storing analog sound signals. A waveform is cut into a spiral groove in a vinyl record. To play the record a needle is dragged through the groove. Digital signals are stored in a variety of ways. Every digital storage method, from CDs to hard drives, uses a series of 1s and 0s.

Analog Storage

These waveforms show two different playbacks of an analog vinyl record.

20. What might cause the slight differences between the two sound waves?

_____

_____

_____

Digital Storage

These waveforms show two playbacks of a digital sound file.

21. Can you observe any differences between the two waveforms? If you noticed differences, what were they? If not, what might that tell you about digital signals?

_____

_____

_____

22. Digital signals have replaced analog signals in many uses. How do you think the differences in analog and digital storage might have affected this change?

_____

_____

_____

Continue Your Exploration

Name: _____ **Date:** _____

Check out the path below or go online to choose one of the other paths shown.

Translating a Binary Signal

- **Hands-On Labs** 👋
- **Test Out Your Own Devices**
- **Propose Your Own Path**

Go online to choose one of these other paths.

Computers receive all their information in the form of digital signals or must first translate information into digital signals in order to use it. Computers use digital signals to store, process, and transmit information. The type of digital signals computers use are binary signals, which are digital signals that vary between two levels. The two levels can be represented as "on," or 1, and "off," or 0. In order for people to read these digital signals, they are often written as a series of 1s and 0s.

Digital Binary Wave

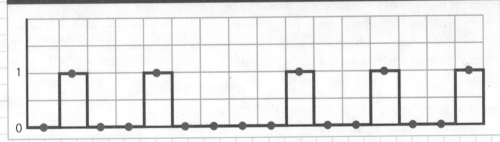

1. Computers translate encoded binary signals into everything you interact with on a computer. Let's see what computers have to do to translate a simple message. In the graph above, each dot represents either a 1 or a 0. Record the pattern of 1s and 0s shown in this signal.

Continue Your Exploration

2. Copy the sequence of 1s and 0s that you recorded on the last page below.

3. Now that you've taken the wave and turned it into a code, use the table to translate the signal into letters that make a word.

It may have taken you a couple of minutes to do this exercise and decode the message. Computers read and interpret codes so fast that it seems to be instantaneous. Many personal computers and even smartphones can perform the task you did, translating an 8-digit code, millions of times per second. That is why they are able to process and communicate so much information, such as changing sound into a digital signal, transmitting the signal, and changing it back to sound without a noticeable delay.

4. How does the ability of a computer to perform so many calculations in a very short time affect how people communicate?

Alphabet in Binary	
Letter	**Binary Code**
A	01000001
B	01000010
C	01000011
D	01000100
E	01000101
F	01000110
G	01000111
H	01001000
I	01001001
J	01001010
K	01001011
L	01001100
M	01001101
N	01001110
O	01001111
P	01010000
Q	01010001
R	01010010
S	01010011
T	01010100
U	01010101
V	01010110
W	01010111
X	01011000
Y	01011001
Z	01011010

5. Collaborate With a partner, create a way that you could send a digital signal using light. Test out your method. What are some of the advantages and disadvantages of your method?

Can You Explain It?

Name: _____   Date: _____

Think again about Internet videos that are viewed millions or even billions of times.

> **How can a video from the Internet appear the same every time you watch it?**

Explore ONLINE!

EVIDENCE NOTEBOOK

Refer to the notes in your Evidence Notebook to help you construct an explanation for why a video from the Internet appears the same every time you view it.

1. State your claim. Make sure your claim fully explains why a video from the Internet appears the same every time you view it.

2. Summarize the evidence you have gathered to support your claim and explain your reasoning.

Checkpoints

Answer the following questions to check your understanding of the lesson.

Use the illustration to answer Questions 3 and 4.

3. The signal represented in the illustration is *an analog / a digital* signal. The variations that occur within the blue bands *are / are not* noise because they are random variations in signal strength. In this type of signal, the variations usually *do / do not* have a large effect on the decoding of the signal.

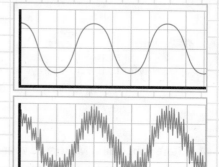

4. This signal is very noisy. Why is the signal still able to transmit information reliably?

    A. Noise cannot change the information in a digital signal.

    B. The noise is not high enough to change any of the values.

    C. The noise causes the amplitude to change too frequently to be detected.

In this illustration, the top waveform represents a transmitted signal and the bottom waveform represents the signal that was received. Use the illustration to answer Questions 5 and 6.

5. Why are these two signals different from one another?

    A. Analog signals are always noisy because they vary continuously.

    B. The process of converting between an analog signal and a digital signal introduced noise.

    C. Noise was introduced by random variations in the signal during the processes of transmitting and receiving the signal.

6. Assume that the received signal is transmitted back to the original point. What is likely to happen to the waveform as it is sent back?

    A. The noise in the returning signal will cancel out the received signal's noise, and the received signal will have the top waveform.

    B. The original noise will remain in the wave and additional noise will be added.

    C. The signal will become noisier, but the information will not be changed.

---

7. Why are digital signals generally better than analog signals for transmitting data over long distances? Choose all that apply.

    A. Digital signals do not use waves, so they do not pick up any noise.

    B. Noise can be removed from a digital signal.

    C. In a digital signal, the level of noise must be high in order for one level to be interpreted as another level.

    D. Digital signals are transmitted faster than analog signals, so there is less chance for noise to be introduced.

Interactive Review

Complete this section to review the main concepts of the lesson.

An analog signal contains continuous information. A digital signal contains information that is represented as a number of values.

A. How can you identify whether a set of information is analog or digital information?

Electromagnetic waves are modulated differently depending on whether analog or digital information is being encoded into the wave.

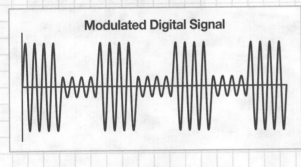

Modulated Digital Signal

B. Compare and contrast a digital modulated wave and an analog modulated wave.

Both analog and digital signals gain noise when they travel from one place to another, but the information in a digital signal is less affected by noise.

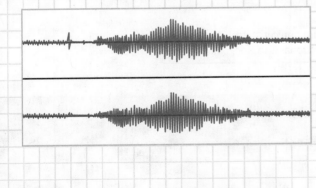

C. Explain why noise has less of an effect on the interpretation of digital signals than on the interpretation of analog signals.

Communication Technology

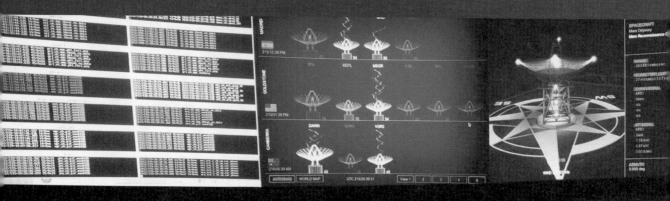

NASA uses a wide variety of communication technologies to do everything from talk with astronauts to store data.

By the end of this lesson . . .

you will be able to analyze the links between signal types, scientific exploration, communication technology.

Go online to view the digital version of the Hands-On Lab for this lesson and to download additional lab resources.

CAN YOU EXPLAIN IT?

Why is the image sent from Mars more clear than the image sent from the moon?

The image on the left was taken from the original broadcast of the moon landing in 1969. This image was transmitted from the moon, through Earth's atmosphere. The image on the right was taken by a rover from the surface of Mars in 2012. This image was transmitted a much farther distance to Earth. The two images were transmitted using different technologies.

1. What are some of the differences that you notice in the clarity of the two images?

2. What do you think could have caused some of these differences in the quality of the two images?

EVIDENCE NOTEBOOK As you explore this lesson, gather evidence to explain the difference in clarity between the two images.

Analyzing the Design of Communication Technology

Either analog or digital information can be encoded into a signal. The signal is then known as either an analog or a digital signal. Analog and digital signals each have specific strengths and weaknesses. When engineers design communication technology, they consider the advantages and disadvantages of each type of signal.

3. Analog and digital signals carry information in different ways. Why would the designers of a communication technology device need to consider the type of signal to use?

Encoding and Decoding Signals

Analog and digital signals are only useful if they can be encoded with information and then decoded. Analog signals can often be encoded and decoded by people or can be encoded and decoded automatically by technology, such as a radio. Analog signals can be used to send simple or complex information that can often be decoded easily.

Digital signals, such as Morse code, can also be encoded and decoded by a person. More complicated signals often require a computer to encode and decode information. A computer can interpret a digital signal millions of times faster than a human, allowing for complex information to be sent and received efficiently. Without a computer, many digital signals would take extremely long times to encode and decode.

Computers make it possible to use digital signals to send and receive complex information.

4. List the advantages of encoding and decoding information using analog and digital signals.

Transmission and Reception of Signals

Digital and analog signals are both used to send information. Analog signals are used in many phone and radio transmissions. Analog signals are useful for applications that do not require perfectly accurate transmission. If noise interferes with an analog radio signal, most of the original message can still be decoded. Digital signals are used when a signal needs to be extremely reliable. When you receive an email, you expect it to be the same message as was originally sent. There is not noise that changes your email. Digital signals can be designed to minimize the effect of noise because they have distinct levels in the signal. However, if there is enough noise that the levels cannot be told apart, the signal can become impossible to decode.

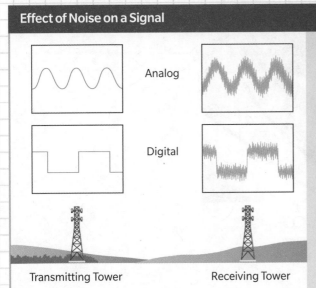

Effect of Noise on a Signal

Analog

Digital

Transmitting Tower

Receiving Tower

Both analog and digital signals pick up noise when they are transmitted. Noise changes the information in an analog signal. Digital signals can be designed so that noise does not have much effect on the signal.

5. Compare analog and digital signal transmission. What are the advantages and disadvantages of each type of signal?

Storage of Information

Information can be stored in both analog and digital forms. Consider a painting and a book. A painting holds a large amount of analog information. Every single part of the painting holds some information. If the paint chips or changes color over time, that information is changed. A book holds digital information, encoded as letters and symbols. A book's pages can yellow over time or be wrinkled, but as long as the letters are still clear, the information stored in the book is unchanged.

This concept applies to any way to store analog or digital information. Vinyl records store analog sound information, but every time the information is accessed, there can be slight differences. Computers can store digital sound information. As long as the computer is not damaged, the information can always be accessed perfectly. However, analog information cannot be perfectly stored digitally. Because analog information is continuous, it cannot be represented digitally without some information being lost.

Analog information can be stored on vinyl records. Any change to the vinyl record, such as a scratch or warping, will change the information stored on the record.

6. Compare analog and digital information storage. What are the advantages and disadvantages of each type of signal?

EVIDENCE NOTEBOOK

7. The moon landing was transmitted as an analog signal and the Mars image was transmitted as a digital signal. How might the type of signal have affected the clarity of the image? Record your evidence.

Understanding Design Choices

When engineers design devices that use signals, the engineers consider the advantages and disadvantages of each signal type. Analog signals can be encoded and decoded without computers. They can be designed to be easy for a human to understand. However, analog signals are not always reliable. The information they contain can be changed during storage, transmission, or processing. Any change to an analog signal changes the information it contains. Digital signals are more reliable. Digital signals can be designed so that noise does not have a large effect on the signal. However, digital signals often require computers in order to encode and decode complex signals.

Curiosity

The Curiosity rover has to send accurate information over extremely long distances. It was designed to transmit digital signals to ensure the reliability of its signals. A car fuel gauge, however, only needs to provide a quick way to see a continuously changing value. It uses an analog signal.

8. For decades, telephones used analog signals to carry messages. Now, many smartphones only use digital signals. What advantages of digital signals could have led to this shift away from the use of analog signals?

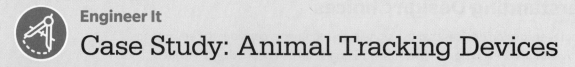

Engineer It

Case Study: Animal Tracking Devices

Scientists use tracking devices to record data about animal movements. They attach devices to wild animals, and then sensors record or transmit data to the scientists. Suppose you want to learn about animal behaviors. You must design a tracking device to collect data on how these animals move.

Shark Tracking Data

Tracking devices can gather data on the average speed of animals such as sharks.

9. Some requirements of the tracking device might be better met by using either an analog or a digital signal. Some requirements may be met by either type of signal and some requirements might not be related to the type of signal at all. On the lines below, write the category that best describes each requirement of the tracking device. A category can be used more than once and some categories may not be used at all.

- Digital signal
- Analog signal
- Either signal type
- Not related to signal type

   A. must be able to transfer information to a computer _____

   B. must accurately store information for long periods of time _____

   C. must be able to withstand weather conditions *Not related to signal type*

   D. must be able to securely remain attached to the animal _____

10. Based on the device's requirements and your answers to the previous question, which type of signal should your device use to process, transfer, and store information? How did you decide which signal to use?

   _____
   _____
   _____
   _____

Exploring Science's Contributions to Communication Technology

We use our knowledge about the natural world as we develop new technology. So as we understand the natural world better, our ability to develop new technologies increases. Often a new scientific discovery leads to advances in several different fields of technology. Think about the devices you use to communicate every day. What scientific discoveries made these devices possible?

Many communication devices run on electric power and use electric signals. Early devices such as this battery enabled researchers to discover ideas that led to our current understanding of electricity. Without this understanding, cell phones, computers, and the Internet would not exist.

11. Which of these statements is an example of scientific knowledge influencing a new technology?

    A. a compact disc providing better music sound quality

    B. newly discovered properties of radio waves being used to encode information

    C. a powerful telescope being used to map the surface of one of Jupiter's moons

    D. computerized timing devices recording a runner's time very accurately

Science and Technology

Technology is the application of science to meet human needs. As our scientific understanding of the world grows, this knowledge often leads to new technologies. If you trace the history of a complicated modern device, you can often see how each new design solution built on previous solutions.

The Development of the Telephone

The modern smartphone was not independently invented. Instead, it was the newest development in a long line of technologies. Look at the timeline below. Trace how the technology that powered the telegraph developed into the smartphones of today.

1837

The first long-distance telegraph message was sent in 1837. Its inventor, Samuel Morse, used scientific knowledge about electric current and magnetism to develop the telegraph. A person sending the message timed the clicks in a digital code. The telegraph used electric signals sent over wires. A series of pulses formed a clicking sound at the receiver. The person on the other end of the line translated these sounds into letters and numbers.

1876

In 1876, Alexander Graham Bell successfully tested the telephone. The telephone improved on the technology of the telegraph. While both devices send electric signals over a wire, the telephone converts the sound waves into an analog wave in an electric current. This wave is then converted back to a sound wave at the receiver's end. By encoding and decoding the sound waves, the telephone did away with the slow process of translating a Morse code message.

12. A practical, widely used telephone was not invented until the telegraph had been in use for several decades. What scientific advance allowed for communication technologies to move beyond the telegraph?

13. What scientific understandings were critical to the development of mobile phones?

1973

Mobile phones first became available in the 1970s thanks to new technology. Using small, inexpensive, and widely available computer chips, mobile phones were able to modulate a wireless signal. The developments that made mobile phones practical were built on understanding the scientific principles of electromagnetic waves and of semiconductor materials, such as silicon, that are used to make computer chips.

2000

In the 2000s, smartphones became widely available. Smartphones and tablets have become an important way for many people to interact. They have even replaced home- or office-based computers for many uses. In addition, deeper understandings of radio waves and encoding methods have increased how quickly information can be sent over radio waves. These advances allow us to stream movies and music to our devices instead of storing them on the devices.

14. **Discuss** With a partner, consider how scientific advances have affected the design and use of technology. Engineers have increased wireless Internet speed because of a better understanding of waves and materials science. How have faster wireless connections affected the role and design of mobile phones?

EVIDENCE NOTEBOOK

15. How might new understandings of the natural world have affected the ways that we send information to Earth from moons and other planets? Record your evidence.

Scientific Advances

Many developments in communication technology have resulted from scientific advances and an understanding of the natural world. As our understanding of the natural world grows, our ability to create technology that makes use of natural phenomena increases. A new scientific discovery can lead to advances in many different fields of technology. Sometimes these new discoveries even lead to the development of technological solutions that had not been previously imagined.

Servers can be used to network many computers together. An understanding of electric current, mathematics, and materials science allow these servers to made.

Relate Science and Technology

16. Why is the development of new technology so closely linked to scientific advances?

_____
_____
_____
_____
_____
_____
_____
_____
_____

17. The invention of new technologies requires an understanding of various scientific fields. Match the technologies on the left with the scientific field or discovery that the technologies made use of on the right.

Computer		Analog Electric Signals
Cell Phone		Electric Current
Telegraph		Semiconductor Chemistry
Telephone		Radio Waves

Analyzing Communication Technology's Relationship to Science

Science plays a key role in the development of new technologies. At the same time, technology helps to advance scientific discovery. As new technologies are developed, they allow us to explore the natural world in ways that were not possible before. Study the images the images. They show how the field of nature recordings has developed through the years.

18. Language SmArts Summarize how technological advances have improved scientists' abilities to study bird vocalizations.

In 1889, Ludwig Koch made the first recording of a bird call onto an Edison wax cylinder. The Edison wax cylinder recorder carved a waveform into a layer of wax. When the player traced the carving, it reproduced the recorded sound.

Koch made his final recording for the British Broadcasting Corporation in 1961 using a magnetic tape recorder in the wild. Many of his early recordings were made using captive birds in recording studios. Advances in recording technology allowed him to take recording equipment into nature.

Advances in technology now allow scientists to make high-quality recordings in the wild. The use of digital signals, improved microphones, and computers to store and analyze information allow for a greater understanding of the calls.

The Effect of Digital Signals on Science

Scientific researchers depend on reliable data to understand the natural world. The invention and use of computers and digital signals have assisted scientific research by making data easier to work with.

19. Which of the following are ways that computers and digital signals would assist in advancing the scientific field? Choose all that apply.

    A. Reliable storage and transmission allow for larger and more cooperative studies to take place.

    B. Reliable storage and transmission allow for wider access to educational resources.

    C. Digital sensors can measure speed, which could not be measured before.

    D. Digital sensors can more reliably transmit data over a distance.

Digital signals have expanded scientists' ability to gather, store, and share data. Digital signals allow scientists to accurately gather information from far away. Digital signals can be used to relay information from oceans, mountaintops, and space, because these signals can be transmitted with high reliability. In addition, with a highly reliable signal, scientists are able to store and share large amounts of data. The ability to store and transfer data allows scientists to work together and to explore areas that were once impossible to explore. Scientists have a greater ability to explore the world due to the reliability of the digital signal.

This remote weather station monitors weather conditions. It then transmits this information using reliable digital signals.

20. Discuss What are some ways in which technology has expanded your ability to communicate information? What are some activities that would be much more difficult if you could not easily communicate with people at a distance?

Hands-On Lab
Explore How Technology Can Improve Scientific Studies

You will make a plan for how to measure the position of a rolling ball over time. Then, you will use your observations to make a plan for how your method could be improved by using newer technologies.

MATERIALS
- meterstick
- small rubber ball
- stopwatch or watch with second hand

Procedure and Analysis

STEP 1 Make a plan for how to measure the distance a ball has rolled after a certain amount of time. Your goal will be to accurately record the ball's position as many times as possible. As the ball rolls, you should record both the ball's position and the time that it is at that position.

STEP 2 **Draw** Write out a procedure for your experiment. Draw a diagram of your experiment's setup to help explain your procedure.

STEP 3 How quickly were you able to accurately record data points? What were some of the major issues that prevented you from capturing more information?

STEP 4 **Draw** Make a plan for how you could use a piece of technology to increase the precision and accuracy of your measurements. Write an explanation of your plan and draw a diagram.

Computers in Science

The invention of digital computers was a huge advance in scientists' ability to study the natural world. Computers can process data very quickly. This allows scientists to examine questions that would have been impossible to explore before computers. For example, to study some models of Earth's climate, millions of calculations are needed to model one day of weather. Creating a long-term model of Earth's climate can take thousands of hours. Without the computer, a large team of scientists would be unable to produce such a model in an entire lifetime. Gathering information over long periods of time has also become possible using computers. This has helped many fields such as astronomy that must have incredibly large amounts of data to generate clear images of objects in space.

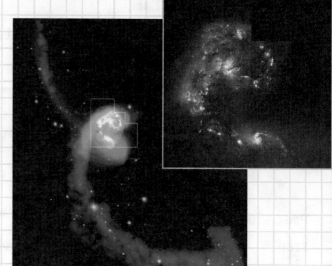

This image was generated using an array of radio telescopes combined with images from the Hubble telescope. The processing of the data in this image was extensive and would be nearly impossible without computers.

21. What are some ways that computers expand our ability to gather information?

EVIDENCE NOTEBOOK

22. How might new technologies have allowed us to transmit clear images to Earth from Mars? Record your evidence.

Do the Math

Analyze Data Collection

23. How might you measure a day's high temperature using an analog thermometer?

Day	High Temp. (°C)
Monday	20
Tuesday	21
Wednesday	23
Thursday	21
Friday	19
Saturday	21
Sunday	20

24. How could measure a day's high temperature using digital devices? How would this process affect the difficulty of gathering large amounts of data?

Continue Your Exploration

Name: _____ **Date:** _____

Check out the path below or go online to choose one of the other paths shown.

Careers in Engineering

- **Hands-On Labs** 👋
- **Studying Space**
- **Propose Your Own Path**

Go online to choose one of these other paths.

Cell Tower Technician

The cell phone, and especially the smartphone, has changed how we communicate. Business, casual conversation, and even scientific study all use cell phones. Cell phones rely on an extensive infrastructure. Landline telephones send information using electric signals that run through wires. The wireless features of cell phones add another step to this process. Cell towers transfer information between individual cellphones and the rest of the phone system. Cell tower technicians help to install, repair, and maintain the infrastructure that allows for cell phones to function.

1. Cell towers receive radio wave signals from cellphones and must convert them into electrical signals. These electric signals are sent over wires to other cell towers. Cell towers can also send and receive digital data from smartphones. What might be some skills that would be useful for a cell tower technician? Choose all that apply.

   A. an understanding of electronics

   B. an understanding of computers

   C. an understanding of chemical engineering

   D. an understanding how radio waves behave

Continue Your Exploration

2. Cell tower technicians often have to install and maintain transmitters and receivers that are attached to tall buildings or cell towers. What might be the advantage of having transmitters and receivers in high places?

3. Cell towers are often placed in busy areas. What might be some considerations when deciding whether an area requires more cell towers? Choose all that apply.

    A. the number of cell phones connecting to each tower

    B. the number of landline telephones in an area

    C. the reception that phones get in an area

4. Cell tower technicians often work on a large number of cell towers. These cell towers form a patchwork to cover a large area. Based on your knowledge of radio signals, why might many cell towers with smaller areas be used instead of a couple towers with much larger areas?

5. **Collaborate** With a partner, make a list of other professions that would require knowledge of communication technology. How would someone working in one of these professions use communication technology?

Can You Explain It?

Name: _____   Date: _____

Take another look at the difference in quality of these images of objects in space.

Why is the image sent from Mars more clear than the image sent from the moon?

 EVIDENCE NOTEBOOK
Refer to the notes in your Evidence Notebook to help you construct an explanation for why the image sent from Mars might be more clear than the image sent from the moon.

1. State your claim. Make sure your claim fully explains why the image sent from Mars might be more clear than the image sent from the moon.

2. Summarize the evidence you have gathered to support your claim and explain your reasoning.

Checkpoints

Answer the following questions to check your understanding of the lesson.

Use the photograph to answer Question 3.

3. This ocean buoy collects data about the water and atmosphere. What are some of the advantages of using digital technology to store and transmit information from the buoy? Choose all that apply.

A. Digital storage devices can store information more accurately than analog storage devices between transmissions.

B. Digital transmissions to distant receivers are more reliable than analog transmissions.

C. Digital sensors on the buoy are more accurate than analog sensors.

4. The Chandra Observatory is a telescope system that orbits high above Earth's surface and observes distant sources of x-rays. Computers on the observatory gather and store information before sending that information to Earth using analog / digital signals. As the signal travels through the atmosphere, random changes will add noise / data / intensity to the signal.

Use the diagram to answer Question 5.

5. Modern computers can process information using digital signals, but not analog signals. In order to make use of an analog signal, a computer must first convert it into a digital signal. Which statement correctly states a reason for this?

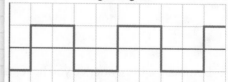

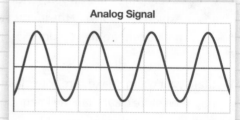

A. Computers process information as a sequence of on and off signals, so they require digital data.

B. The changes in analog signals occur too slowly for a computer to process.

C. Digital data does not require as much storage space and memory as analog data.

6. Since the development of the computer, many new models of natural phenomena have been developed. Why might these models not have been developed before the computer was widely available? Choose all that apply.

A. Computers allowed scientists to collect new data that led to new models.

B. Before computers, models of natural phenomena were not thought of as useful.

C. The calculations required for the models could not be done without computers.

D. Models of natural phenomena were never accurate before computers.

Interactive Review

Complete this section to review the main concepts of the lesson.

Depending on the purpose of a technology, an analog or a digital signal may be preferred.

A. Make a table to compare and contrast how digital and analog signals work in communication technology.

Scientific advances have contributed to the development of communication technology.

B. Give at least two examples to show how scientific advances can lead to new or improved communication technology.

New communication technologies increase the ability of scientists to study, model, and explore the natural world and collaborate with each other.

C. Describe ways that new communication technologies have changed the way scientists can work.

Choose one of the activities to explore how this unit connects to other topics.

☐ Life Science Connection

Sensing Waves Living organisms must gather, interpret, and respond to information from their environment. Eyes and ears have specialized structures for this function.

Research how the human eye and ear interact with waves to gather information. Then extend your research to examine how structures for sight and hearing function differently in an animal than in humans. Make a multimedia presentation to share what you learn with the class.

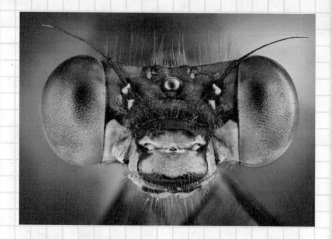

☐ Technology Connection

Signal Transformation Information transfer technologies often receive one type of signal and change it into another. For example, a radio receives electromagnetic radio wave signals and transforms them into electrical signals. Speakers convert the electrical signals into sound waves in air.

Conduct research to learn how an information technology you use daily converts signals from one form to another, and summarize what you learn in a well-written paragraph. Explain how engineers design the device to minimize loss of signal clarity while performing signal transformations.

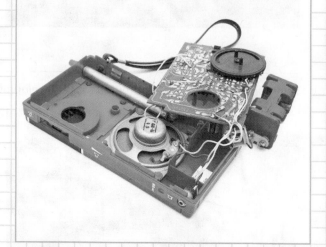

☐ Social Studies Connection

When Radio Made Waves The first radio station in the United States began broadcasting in 1920 from the top of the Westinghouse Electric factory in Pittsburgh. Within five years, there were more than 500 broadcasting stations in America. Radio changed many aspects of American culture.

Research how radio, or another information technology, influenced American society, including family life, politics, consumer advertising, the entertainment industry, and international awareness. Make a poster explaining American culture before and after the invention to share your findings.

Name: _____   Date: _____

Complete this review to check your understanding of the unit.

Use the graphs of the songbird wave patterns to answer Questions 1–2.

1. Birds, like humans, modulate waves when producing sound. What wave components do songbirds modulate when singing? Select all that apply.

   A. speed

   B. frequency

   C. amplitude

   D. wavelength

2. The audible portions of birdsong cover a range of frequencies. Birdsong is a type of digital / analog information.

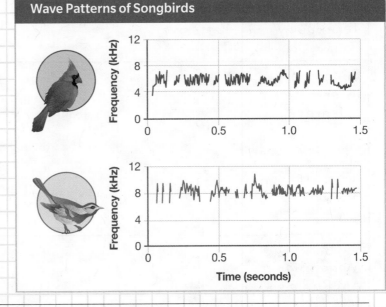

Wave Patterns of Songbirds

3. Which scenarios are examples of noise? Select all that apply.

   A. raindrops making ripples on a lake surface

   B. a sunset obscuring your view of a sailboat

   C. chatty neighbors talking over the teacher

   D. trouble finding the light switch in a dark room

4. Digital waves

   A. can be encoded with frequency and amplitude modulations.

   B. are equally affected by noise as are analog waves.

   C. can be encoded with amplitude modulations only.

   D. are less effective in computer-based technologies than analog waves.

Use the image of the satellite antenna to answer Question 5.

5. This large radio antenna is directed out into space. What type of signal is it most likely to use?

   A. analog sound waves

   B. digital sound waves

   C. analog electromagnetic waves

   D. digital electromagnetic waves

Name: _____   **Date:** _____

6. Complete the table by providing brief explanations of how the topic and technology pairs relate to each big concept.

Topic / Technology Pair	Patterns	Structure and Function
Encoding Information / Telegraph		
Wave Modulation / AM Radio		
Digital Signals / Binary Code		
Noise / Tape Recorder		

Use the piano keyboard image to answer Questions 7–10.

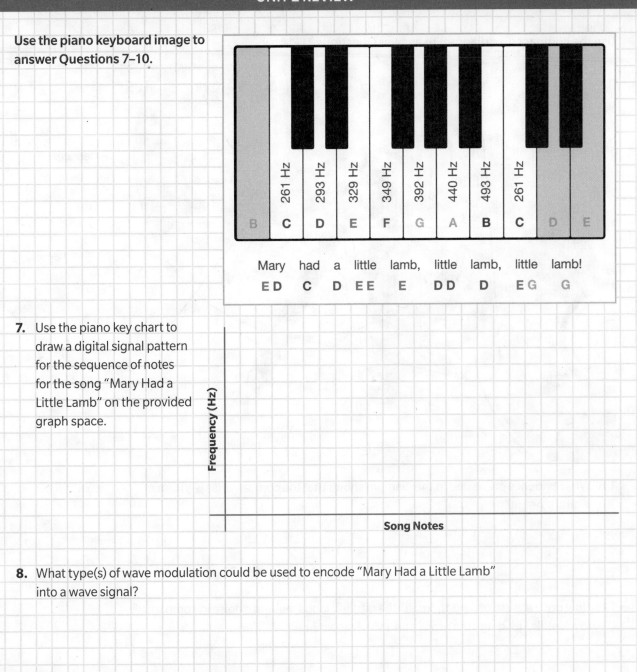

B	C	D	E	F	G	A	B	C	D	E
	261 Hz	293 Hz	329 Hz	349 Hz	392 Hz	440 Hz	493 Hz	261 Hz		

Mary had a little lamb, little lamb, little lamb!
E D   C   D E E   E   D D   D   E G   G

Frequency (Hz)

Song Notes

7. Use the piano key chart to draw a digital signal pattern for the sequence of notes for the song "Mary Had a Little Lamb" on the provided graph space.

8. What type(s) of wave modulation could be used to encode "Mary Had a Little Lamb" into a wave signal?

9. If a child sang "Mary Had a Little Lamb" along with the piano notes, would an analog or a digital recording of the song be better? Make a claim and provide evidence to support your reasoning.

10. Explain one way that noise could be introduced to a radio transmission of this song.

Use the compact disc diagram to answer Questions 11–14.

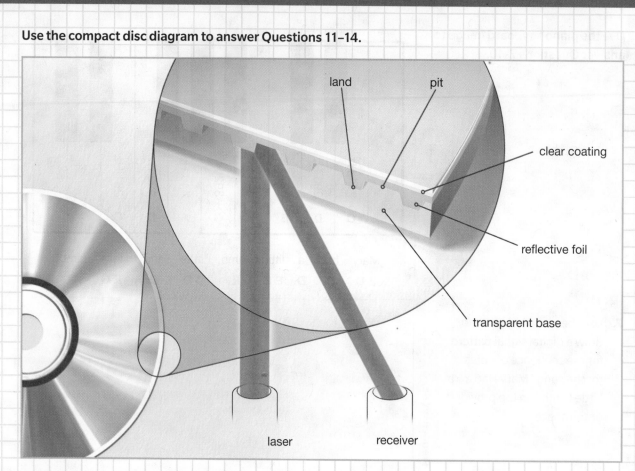

11. What evidence presented in the diagram shows that the compact disc is a form of digital storage?

12. How does the use of light to "read" the pits and lands minimize noise in comparison to a needle "reading" the groove on a vinyl record?

13. What big ideas about waves did engineers need to know to develop CD technology?

14. CD technology became obsolete with the development of Internet-based audio storage, including MP3 files. How does bypassing material storage of digital recordings (on a CD or vinyl record) provide advantages to music-loving consumers?

Name: _____   Date: _____

How can laser tag be improved?

An innovative laser tag company surveyed its clients about possible improvements to their facility and found that consumers want more high-tech challenges. One consumer said, "I want to tag people without having them in my line of sight, like around corners, or through waterfalls and one-way mirrors." Another suggested the company provide players with a way to send laser messages in outdoor, wooded environments during team-on-team battles.

As a member of the company's game design team, you are tasked with investigating the feasibility of implementing the consumers' suggestions. Is it possible to send a decodable, laser-light message around two opaque barriers and through two different translucent materials without losing the quality of the signal? Evaluate the results of your research on the feasibility of this task and make design recommendations in a report to company leadership.

The steps below will help guide your research and develop your recommendation.

Engineer It

1. **Define the Problem** With your team, write a statement defining the problem you have been asked to solve. How will you encode a message into laser light? What are the criteria and constraints involved in successfully sending a laser light message past obstacles and through different materials?

Engineer It

2. **Conduct Research** Research the light transmission properties of at least three different materials for building obstacles for your course. How will light be absorbed or reflected by different barriers? Investigate which materials will allow clear transmission of your light message while giving players an exciting challenge.

3. **Analyze and Evaluate Research** Determine which materials work best for sending light messages. What other factors will you need to consider when evaluating materials for building your course?

4. **Identify and Recommend a Solution** Use what you learned from your research to make recommendations for a full-scale laser tag facility. Create a diagram to illustrate your recommendations. How will you use your knowledge of light behavior to justify your design recommendations?

5. **Communicate** Work with your team to prepare a report of your facility recommendations based on your research. Use your diagram to explain your recommendations. Include evidence showing how your final design solution addressed the criteria and constraints you defined for the problem.

✓ Self-Check

	I identified the criteria and constraints involved in sending and receiving a light-encoded message.	
	I analyzed research for ways to direct light around and through barriers.	
	I evaluated research to make design recommendations, taking the interests of the company into account.	
	I linked relevant evidence to recommendations in my report.	

Glossary

Pronunciation Key							
Sound	**Symbol**	**Example**	**Respelling**	**Sound**	**Symbol**	**Example**	**Respelling**
ă	a	pat	PAT	ŏ	ah	bottle	BAHT'l
ā	ay	pay	PAY	ō	oh	toe	TOH
âr	air	care	KAIR	ô	aw	caught	KAWT
ä	ah	father	FAH•ther	ôr	ohr	roar	ROHR
är	ar	argue	AR•gyoo	oi	oy	noisy	NOYZ•ee
ch	ch	chase	CHAYS	o͞o	u	book	BUK
ĕ	e	pet	PET	o͞o	oo	boot	BOOT
ĕ (at end of a syllable)	eh	settee lessee	seh•TEE leh•SEE	ou	ow	pound	POWND
ĕr	ehr	merry	MEHR•ee	s	s	center	SEN•ter
ē	ee	beach	BEECH	sh	sh	cache	CASH
g	g	gas	GAS	ŭ	uh	flood	FLUHD
ĭ	i	pit	PIT	ûr	er	bird	BERD
ĭ (at end of a syllable)	ih	guitar	gih•TAR	z	z	xylophone	ZY•luh•fohn
ī	y eye (only for a complete syllable)	pie island	PY EYE•luhnd	z	z	bags	BAGZ
îr	ir	hear	HIR	zh	zh	decision	dih•SIZH•uhn
j	j	germ	JERM	ə	uh	around broken focus	uh•ROWND BROH•kuhn FOH•kuhs
k	k	kick	KIK	ər	er	winner	WIN•er
ng	ng	thing	THING	th	th	thin they	THIN THAY
ngk	ngk	bank	BANGK	w	w	one	WUHN
				wh	hw	whether	HWETH•er

absorption (uhb•SOHRP•shuhn)
in optics, the transfer of light energy to particles of matter (63)
absorción   en la óptica, la transferencia de energía luminosa a las partículas de materia

amplitude (AM•plih•tood)
the maximum distance that the particles of a wave's medium vibrate from their rest position (13)
amplitud   la distancia máxima a la que vibran las partículas del medio de una onda a partir de su posición de reposo

analog signal (AN•uh•lawg SIG•nuhl)
a signal whose properties can change continuously in a given range (109)
señal análoga   una señal cuyas propiedades cambian continuamente en un rango determinado

digital signal (DIJ•ih•tl SIG•nuhl)
a signal that can be represented as a sequence of discrete values (109)
señal digital   una señal que se puede representar como una secuencia de valores discretos

encode (en•KOHD)
to convert information from one form into another for the purpose of communication (93)
codificar   convertir información de una forma a otra con el propósito de lograr la comunicación

frequency (FREE•kwuhn•see)
the number of cycles, or vibrations, per unit of time; also the number of waves produced in a given amount of time (15)
frecuencia   número de ciclos, o vibraciones, por unidad de tiempo; también el número de ondas producidas en un tiempo dado

light (LYT)
a form of radiant electromagnetic energy that can be seen by the human eye (42)
luz   una forma de energía electromagnética radiante que es visible para el ojo humano

mechanical wave (mih•KAN•ih•kuhl WAYV)
a wave that requires a medium through which to travel (24)
onda mecánica   una onda que requiere un medio para desplazarse

medium (MEE•dee•uhm)
for waves, the material through which a wave can travel (24)
medio   para las ondas, el medio a través del cual se desplaza una onda

noise (NOYZ)
an unwanted change to a signal (112)
ruido   cambio no deseado a una señal

reflection (rih•FLEK•shuhn)
the bouncing back of a ray of light, sound, or heat when the ray hits a surface that it does not go through (64)
reflexión   el rebote de un rayo de luz, sonido o calor cuando el rayo golpea una superficie pero no la atraviesa

refraction (rih•FRAK•shuhn)
the bending of a wave front as the wave front passes between two substances in which the speed of the wave differs (65)
refracción   el curvamiento de un frente de ondas a medida que el frente pasa entre dos sustancias en las que la velocidad de las ondas difiere

signal (SIG•nuhl)
anything that serves to direct, guide, or warn (93)
señal   cualquier cosa que sirve para dirigir, guiar o advertir

sound wave (SOWND WAYV)
a longitudinal wave that is caused by vibrations and that travels through a material medium (27)
onda sonora   una onda longitudinal que se origina debido a vibraciones y que se desplaza a través de un medio material

T–Z

transmission (trans•MISH•uhn)

the passing of light or other form of energy through matter (63)

transmisión el paso de la luz u otra forma de energía a través de la materia

wave (WAYV)

a periodic disturbance in a solid, liquid, or gas as energy is transmitted through a medium (6)

onda una perturbación periódica en un sólido, líquido o gas que se transmite a través de un medio en forma de energía

wavelength (WAYV•lengkth)

the distance from any point on a wave to the corresponding point on the next wave (13)

longitud de onda la distancia entre cualquier punto de una onda y el punto correspondiente de la siguiente onda

wave speed (WAYV SPEED)

the speed at which a wave travels through a medium (15)

rapidez de onda la rapidez a la cual viaja una onda a través de un medio

Index

Page numbers for key terms are in **boldface** type.
Page numbers in *italic* type indicate illustrative material, such as photographs, graphs, charts and maps.

A

absorption, 63
  of color of light waves, 49, *49*,
    55–56, *55*, 67–69, *70*
  of colors of light, *49*
  frequency and, 31
  of light, 63, 79
  of mechanical waves, 31, *31*
acoustic panel, 36
act, 66
air, 28
  frequency of sound in, *28*
alphabet in binary code, 120, *120*
amplitude, 13, *13*
  of all waves, 13, 21, 51
  of analog and digital signals, 110
  of blast waves, 13
  calculation of, 16
  encoding information into EM
    waves, 98, *98*, 101, 105
  energy related to, *15*, 15–16, 52
  light intensity and, 51, *51*
  of light waves, 47, 51, *51*, 59
  of mechanical waves, 29
  at a point in space, *30*, 30–31, *31*
  relationship to wavelength and
    frequency, 48
  of spreading waves, 39, *39*
  of waves at media boundaries, 34
**amplitude modulation, 99, *99*, 101,
    105**
**analog signal, 106–120, 109, *109*,
    110, 118**
  advantage of, 126, *126*, 127, 129
  effect on science, *136*
  encoding and decoding, 128
  encoding into electromagnetic
    waves, 113, *113*, 114
  graphing, 110, *110*, 111, *111*
  noise in, 117, *117*, 118
  storage noise, 118, *118*

  storage on vinyl records, 118, 127,
    127
  storage types, 118
  thermometers, 108, *108*
  transmission noise, 118, *118*
  as waves, *110*
analysis
  of amplitude and brightness, 53
  of available light, 50, *50*
  of communication methods, 89, 95
  of composition of rock, 126
  by computers, 135, 138, 140
  of digital information, 138
  of format changes in audio
    recordings, 118
  of investigations, 11, 26, 53, 73, 88,
    113, 116, 137
  of a kaleidoscope, 65, *65*
  of light's effect on sight, 67–71, *70*,
    77
  of sound volume, 31
  of types of waves in earthquakes, 12
  of volume of sound, 31
animals, production of light, 42
animal senses, 23, 80, *80*
animal tracking device, 129, *129*
argument, 76
Assessment
  Lesson Self-Check, 19–21, 37–39,
    57–59, 77–79, 103–105, 121–123,
    141–143
  Unit Performance Task, 85–86,
    149–150
  Unit Review, 81–84, 145–148
astronaut, 87, *87*, 124
astronomy, 138–139
atmosphere, 45, *45*

B

behavior
  of amplitude, 104
  of light waves, 60–76

  of mechanical waves, 22–36
Bell, Alexander Graham, 132
binary alphabet, *120*
binary code, 112, *112*, 120, *120*
**binary digital signal, *111*, 112, *119*,
    119–120**
blast wave, 13, *13*, 16
boundary
  behavior of waves at media
    boundaries, *32*, *33*, *34*
**boundary, behavior of waves at
    media boundaries, 32–34**
brightness, *51*, 53–54, 59, *59*

C

calculation of amplitude, 16
**Can You Explain It?, 5, 19, 23, 37, 41,
    57, 61, 77, 91, 103, 107, 121, 125,
    141**
Careers in Engineering, 139–140
carrier wave, 113–114
cause
  of mechanical waves, 27, 31
  of tsunami, 24
cell phones, 97, *129*
Chandra Observatory, 125
change
  in amplitude of sound waves, 31
  in analog waves, 126
  bounce of sound waves as, 36
  of brightness of light, 55, *55*
  of energy and amplitude, *15*, 16
  of format of audio devices, 118
  in frequency, wavelength, amplitude
    of waves, 48
  modulation of, *113*
  modulation of waves, 99, *99*,
    109–110, 113–114, *114*, 115,
    115, 117
  noise in a signal as, 114–118, *117*
  of path of light, 64, *64*
  of properties of waves, 99–100, *100*

of speed of light waves, *67*

in speed of sound, 27, *27*

of variables in visible spectrum, 47,
47

in wavelength and speed of waves,
34

Checkpoints, 20, 38, 58, 78, 104, 122,
142

cloud storage, 133

Collaborate, 14, 18, 36, 56, 76, 95,
102, 120, 140

color

addition of, *70, 70–71, 71*

of light, *47, 48, 48, 49, 50, 59, 59*

perception of, *66, 66, 67–69, 70, 70*

primary and secondary colors of
light, *71, 71*

of visible light, 47–50

color addition, *70, 70–71, 71*

combined waves, 11

communication

over long distances, 92–95, *93,* 103,
103

with signals, 93–95, *93, 95*

types of, 93

communication technology, 90, *90,*
124–140

analyzing the design of, *126,*
126–130, *127, 128, 129*

relationship to science, 135–138

science's contribution to, 131–134,
135

in twentieth century, 97, *97*

compression, 11, *11*

computer

data collection with, 138

encoding and decoding of
information, 95

interpretation of signals, 128, *128*

role in scientific research, 136

in science, 138

sending and receiving information,
97

storage of data, 127

use of binary digit signals, 111, 112,
119–120

concave lens, 69, *69*

conclusion, drawing, 7, 50, 53

Connecting Evidence, 53

convex lens, 68, *68*

cosmic ray, 43, *43*

crest

of light waves, 51

of waves, 11, *11*

cycle of waves, *13,* 13–15, *14, 15*

D

data

coding of, 126

collection of, 126, *126,* 135, 136,
138, 140

computer processing of, 136–138

evaluation of, 150

from Hubble Telescope and Chandra
X-Ray Observatory, 125, *125*

recording and transmission of, 129,
129, 136, *136*

storage of, 124, 136

decoding, 93–95, 128

design of communication devices,
126, 126–133, *127, 128, 129, 130,*
132, 133

design process, 85–86, 149–150

diagram, 20, 58

ray diagram, 64, *64*

of technologies, 134

of tsunami, *8*

Venn, *56*

wave diagrams, 99, *99, 102, 104*

of waves, 142

difference

between analog and digital signals,
10, 108, *108*

in light and ability to see, 50, *50*

between longitudinal and
transverse waves, 9, 11, 21, *21*

noise causing in signals, 115, 117,
117, 118, *118*

in quality of signals, 141, *141*

between sound and light waves,
46, *46*

digital binary wave, *119,* 119–120

digital sensor, *126*

digital signal

advantages of, 126, 127, 129

analysis of, 138

binary digital signal, *111,* 112, *119,*
119–120

effect on science, 136

encoding and decoding, 128

encoding into electromagnetic
waves, 114, *114*

noise in, 117, *117*

storage noise, 118, *118*

translate a digital signal, 115

translating, 115

direction of light through a medium,
66, 67, *67*

Discuss, 7, 11, 13, 27, 30, 42, 68, 94,
133, 136

distance

analog and digital signal noise and,
118, *118*

communication over, 91–95, *93,*
97, *97*

dolphin, 1, *1,* 23, 31, *31*

domino, 5, *5,* 19, *19*

Do the Math, 15, 44, 48, 99

Analyze Digital Information, 138

Calculate the Amplitude of a Wave,
16

Number of Levels in a Signal, 111

Practice Drawing Ray Diagrams, 64

Draw, 28, 49, 54, 64, 137

drum patterns, 93, *93*

E

earthquake

tsunami caused by, 24

waves of, *9,* 9–10, 12, *12,* 25, 29, *29*

echo, 32, *32,* 33, 35–36, *36*

Edison wax cylinder, 135, *135*

effect

of earthquakes, 24

of vibration, 27, 31

electret microphone, 17

electrical signal, 97, *97,* 131, 144

electric field, 42

electromagnetic (EM) spectrum, 42,
43, *43*

electromagnetic (EM) waves, 42, *43*

animals sensing, 80, *80*

blocked by atmosphere, 45, *45*

communication technology using, 97, 97–98, *98*, 105, *105*

encoding information into, 98, *98*, *113*, 113–114, *114*

light waves as, 59

medium for travel, 42, 44, *44*, 46

modulation of, 99, 99–102, *100*, 110, 113–114

path of, 63–64

radar and, 80

radio conversion of, 144

radio waves, 98, *98*

relationship of energy with frequency and wavelength, 44

safety of, 44, 46

source of, 45

speed of, 44, *44*

vibration of, 42, *42*

encoding, 93

analog and digital signals, 128

digital and analog information into EM waves, *113*, 113–114, *114*

information, 93–95, 98, *98*, 99, *100*, 105

energy

absorption and reflection of, 55–56

amplitude of waves and, *15*, 15–16, 29, 34, 52, 59, *59*

of blast waves, 13, *13*, 16

brightness of light and, 53–54, 55, 59, *59*, 67

carried in a medium, 24, *24*

change of form, 55

conversion of light to thermal energy, 55–56

conversion of wave energy to thermal energy, 31

of electromagnetic waves, 42, 44, *45*, 45–46

frequency and, *45*

light, 40, *40*, *41*, 42, 42–46, 105

of mechanical waves, *29*, 29–31, *30*, 39, *39*

relationship with frequency and wavelength, 44–46

of sound, 96

of spreading waves, 30–31, *30–31*

transfer by waves, 5–8

transfer of light from matter, 63

transferred in waves, 5, *6*, 6–8, *7*, 11, *11*, 19, *19*, 21, *21*, 24, *24*, 42, *42*, 96

of water waves, 6

in waves, 13

of waves at boundaries of media, 32–34

engineering

animal tracking devices, 129, *129*

audio recorder, 118

communication devices, 97, *97*, 126

design for use of sunlight, 74, *74*

design of soundproof rooms, 35–36

devices for information transmission and storage, 129

Internet speed, 133

medical equipment, 34, *34*

periscopes, 75, *75*

sound recordings, 100, *100*

Engineer It, 15, 46

Case Study: Animal Tracking Devices, 130

Compare Communication Methods, 98

Connection: Signal Transformation, 144

Engineering Solutions to Light Pollution, 71

Explain Recorded Audio, 100, *100*

Explain Reliability in Signal Storage, 118, *118*

Explore Mechanical Waves in Medicine, 34

Performance Task, 85–86, 149–150

Propose a Solution Using Sunlight, 74

equation for wave speed, 15

evidence

connecting, 53

supporting claims, 19, 37, 57, 77, 103, 121, 141

Evidence Notebook, 5, 8, 12, 19, 23, 26, 34, 37, 41, 44, 49, 57, 61, 65, 71, 77, 91, 97, 103, 107, 112, 121, 125, 128, 133, 138, 141

Exploration

Analyzing Analog and Digital Information, 108–111

Analyzing Communication Technology's Relationship to Science, 135–138

Analyzing How Light Affects What We See, 67–71

Analyzing Human Perception of Light Waves, 47–50

Analyzing Mechanical Waves and Energy, 29–32

Analyzing the Design of Communication Technology, 126–130

Analyzing Waves in Communication, 96–98

Comparing Longitudinal and Transverse Waves, 9–12

Explaining How Noise Affects Signals, 115–118

Explaining the Behavior of Waves at Media Boundaries, 32–34

Exploring How Signals Gain Noise, 116–120

Exploring Interactions of Light and Matter, 62–66

Exploring Long-Distance Communication, 92–95

Exploring Science's Contribution to Communication Technology, 131–134

Exploring the Nature of Light, 42–46

Exploring Waves, 5–8

Identifying the Properties of Waves, 13–16

Investigating How Waves Are Modified, 99–100

Investigating Light as Transverse Waves, 51–54

Investigating Mechanical Waves, 24–28

Using Light to Solve Problems, 72–74

Explore ONLINE! 6, 7, 20, 25, 29, 30, 32, 33, 34, 42, 46, 68, 69, 96, 99, 107, 121

explosion, 13, *13*, 16, *16*

F

fault, 8, *8*
filter, 70, 73
fire signals, 93
formula for amplitude, 15
frequency, 15
  absorption and, 31
  of analog and digital signals, 110
  color of light and, 47, 47–48, *48*
  of electromagnetic waves, 43, *43*, 44, 46
  encoding information into EM waves, 101, 105
  of light waves, 47, *47*
  media and, 28, *28*, 34, *34*
  relationship to wavelength and amplitude, 48
  wave period and, 14, *14*
  wave speed and, 15
frequency modulation, 99, *99*, 101, 105
friction, 31

G

gamma ray, 43, *43*, 45, *45*
graph
  of absorption of waves, *31*
  of digital binary wave, *119*
  of digital waves, *111*
  of encoded analog information, *113*
  of encoded digital information, *114*
  of light waves, *58*
  of mass of a glass of water (analog information), *110*
  of mechanical waves, *30*
  of noise in a signal, 115, *115, 117*
  of sharks' speed, 129, *129*
  of wave properties, 13, *13*, 14, *14*, 20, 21, *21*
  of waves, *11, 12, 20, 21, 21, 28, 43, 45, 48, 51, 52, 73, 104, 105, 122, 137*

H

Hands-On Lab
  Encode a Message, 94–95
  Explore How Technology Can Improve Scientific Studies, 137–138
  Generate Mechanical Waves, 26–27
  Investigate Waves, 14
  Light Up a Maze, 73–74
  Make a Penny Disappear, 67
  Model Specific Wave Properties, 52–54
  Model Two Types of Waves, 10–11
  Transmit and Record a Signal, 116–117
Hubble Telescope, 125, 139
humans' perception of light waves, 47–50

I–J

identify
  media, 28
  signal types, 112
information
  on AM and FM radio, 101–102, *102*
  in analog and digital form, *108*, 108–111, *110, 111*, 123, *123*, 143, *145*
  analysis of digital information, 138
  computer processing of, 106, *106*, 137–138, *138*
  design of equipment, 126–133
  encoding and decoding, 93–100, *99*
  long-distance communication of, 92–95, 105, 136, *136*
  modification of waves carrying, 99, 99–100, *100*, 105, *105*
  noise affecting transfer of, *114, 115*, 115–118, *116, 117, 118*, 123, *123*
  storage in analog and digital form, 127
  transfer in waves, 96–98, *105*
  translation of binary signals, *119*, 119–120, *120*
information transfer technology, 96, *142*

K

kaleidoscope, 65, *65*
Koch, Ludwig, 135

L

Language SmArts, 9, 25, 45, 96, 110, 135
  Apply Your Knowledge of Wave Energy and Amplitude, 16
laser tag, *149*, 149–150
lens
  convex and concave, 68–69
  in periscopes, *75*, 75–76
  refraction of light, 73
Lesson Self-Check, 19–21, 37–39, 57–59, 77–79, 103–105, 121–123, 141–143
Life Science Connection
  Animal Wave Senses, 80
  Sensing Waves, 144
light, 42
  absorption of, 63, *63*
  brightness, 52–53, 54, 59, *59*
  change to thermal energy, 55
  color perception, 47, 47–50, *48, 49, 50*, 59, *59*, 67–69, *70*
  as energy, 42–46
  interactions with matter, 62–66
  mediums and, 60, *60*
  path of, 63–64
  problem solving with, 72–74, 79
  reflection of, 61, *61*, 62, 64, *64*
  refraction of, *66, 67*, 66–67
  sight and, 67–71, *67*
  sources of, 42
  speed of, 44, *44*, 66, 67
  from the sun, 41, *41*, 89
  transmission of, 66, *66*

infrared wave, 43, *43*
interaction of light and matter, 40, *40*, 49, *49*, 62, 62–71, *63, 64, 66, 67, 70, 77*
Interactive Review, 21, 39, 59, 79, 105, 123, 143

transparent materials and, 40, *40*

visible, 42, 67–68

light bulb, 54

lighthouses, 96

light pollution, 71

Light Reflectance Value (LRV), 56, *56*

light signal, 93, *93*

light wave, 1, 3, *3*, 40–56

behavior of, 60–76

color of, 47, 47–48, *48*

as electromagnetic waves, 42, 59

human perception of, 47–50

predicting the path of, 87, 89

sound waves compared to, 46, *46*

as transverse waves, *51*, 51–54

See also **electromagnetic (EM)
waves.**

longitudinal wave

in earthquakes, 12, *12*

as mechanical waves, 25, *25*

motion of, *9*, 9–12, *11*, 21, *21*

transfer of energy, 11, *11*

lumen, 53–54

M

magnetic field, 42

magnetic tape recorder, 135, *135*

Mars Curiosity rover, 129, *129*

material

effect on speed of light, 44, *44*, 67,
67

effect on speed of sound waves, 27,
27, 36

interaction with light, 40, *40*, 62,
62–71, *63*, *64*, *66*, 67, *70*, *77*

mechanical waves in, 24, 24–25, *25*

See also **medium.**

matter

absorption of light, 63

changing path of light, 64, *64*

electromagnetic waves and, 59, 68

interaction of light and, 62–66

motion of waves, 25

transfer of light energy to, 63

transmission of light, 63, *63*, 66, *66*

waves and, 6, *6*, 24, 39

See also **material; objects.**

measurement

of composition of rock, 126

with computers, 137–138

Light Reflectance Value (LRV), 56, *56*

of rolling ball speed, 137

with sound waves, 23, *23*

of speed of sharks, 129, *129*

using analog instruments, 109, *109*,
127, *127*

using digital sensors, 126, *126*

of wave properties, 52, 52–53

mechanical wave, 22–36, **24**

absorption of, 31, *31*

amplitude and energy of, 29, *52*,
52–54

behavior at media boundaries,
32–34, 39, *39*

in earthquakes, 12, *12*, 29, *29*

generation of, 26–27

mapping seafloor with, 23, *23*, 37, *37*

in medicine, 34, *34*

necessity of a medium, *24*, 24–25,
39, 46

sound waves, 27, *27*

spread of, 30, *30*

transverse and longitudinal waves,
25, *25*

visualization using, 23, *23*

See also **longitudinal wave;
sound wave; transverse wave.**

media boundaries, 32, 32–34, *33*, *34*,
39, *39*

medicine, ultrasound imaging, 34, *34*

medium, 24

absorption of waves, 31, *31*

for earthquakes, 12

electromagnetic (EM) waves and,
46, *46*

light waves and, 41, 42, 44, *44*, 46,
59, 66, *66*

mechanical waves in, 24, 24–25, 31,
39, *39*

movement of waves through, 9, 12,
12

opaque, translucent, transparent,
63, *63*

refraction of light in, 67, *67*

sound waves and, 46, *46*

wave frequency and, 28, *28*

wavelength and, 28, *28*

wave path in, *30*, 30–31

wave speed and, 27, *27*

methods of communication, 89

microwave, 43, *43*, 90

millimeter wave, 43, *43*

mirror

for lighting around corners, 72–73

in periscopes, 75, 75–76

reflection of light, 64, *64*, 74, *74*

model/modeling

development and use of, 86, 150

light and sound, 3

waves, 10–11

modulation, 99–102

of analog and digital signals, 110

encoding analog and digital
information, *113*, 113–114, *114*

of radio waves, 114, *114*

Morse, Samuel, 93

Morse code, 95, *95*

motion/movement

of mechanical waves, 24, 24–25, *25*

of tectonic plates, 8, *8*, 9, *9*, 29, *29*

tracking animal movements, 129,
129

of waves, 9–12, *11*, *12*, 25, 31, 39,
39, 100, *100*

music, 80, *80*

Music Connection

Controlling Sound Waves to Make
Music, 80

N

NASA, 124, *124*, 125

near infrared wave, 43, *43*

nearsightedness, 69

New Horizons spacecraft, 91, *91*,
103, *103*

noise

in analog and digital signals, *115*,
115–118, *117*, *118*

digital signals' minimizing, 126

distance's effect on, 123, *123*, 126

O

objects

capturing images of objects in space, 125, *125*, *138*, 139–140, *141*

dolphin's ability to locate objects, 31

light and ability to see, 23, *23*, *64*, 64–71, 66, 70, 77

perception of color of, *49*, 49–50, *50*, 59, *59*, 67–69, 70, 79

reflection of sound, 37, *37*

refraction of light, 66, *66*, 70, 77

transparent, translucent, and opaque, *49*, *50*, 55–56, *56*, *64*, *64*, 70

in waves, 6, *6*

observations, 7, 10, 13, 26, 46, 52–53, 137

ocean wave

as mechanical waves, 25, *25*

movement of energy, 24

transfer of energy, 4, *4*, 6, 24

tsunami, 8, *8*, 24

online activities, 6, 7, 20, 25, 29, 30, 32, 33, 34, 42, 46, 68, 69, 96, 99, 107, 121

opaque materials, 63, *63*

optical illusions, 67, *67*

P–Q

partial reflection and transmission, *33*, *33*, *39*, *39*

particles, vibration in waves, 9

patterns

of colors in rainbow, 47, *47*

in kaleidoscope, 65, *65*

signals as, 93–95

See also **waves.**

People in Science, 17–18

period of waves, *13*, 13–15, 21

periscopes, *75*, 75–76

Pluto, 91

precision of measurements, 137

prediction, 55, 104

primary and secondary colors of light, *71*

primary colors of light, 70

prism, 48, *48*, 66, *66*, 73

problem solving with light, 72–74, 79

procedure

Encode a Message, 94–95

Explore How Technology Can Improve Scientific Studies, 137–138

Generate Mechanical Waves, 26–27

Light Up a Maze, 73–74

Model Specific Wave Properties, *52*, 52–54

Model Two Types of Waves, 10–11

Transmit and Record a Signal, 116–117

process

design process, 85–86, 149–150

transmission of mechanical waves, 32

properties

of analog and digital signals, 109–110, *110*, 128

of electromagnetic waves, *98*, 98–100, *99*, *100*

modeling wave properties, *52*, 52–54

modulation of, *99*, *99*

of waves, *13*, 13–16, *14*, *15*, 21, *21*, *98*, *98*

of waves at media boundaries, 34

proportion of energy to amplitude, 15, 16, 21

R

radar, 80, *80*

radio

first broadcasts, 144

modulation of waves, 100

transfer of information, 97, *97*

use of analog waves, 110

radio telescope, 138

radio wave

AM and FM, 101–102

development of radios and, 144

effect of noise, 115

energy of, 44

frequencies and wavelengths of, 43

frequencies of, *43*

frequency and distance traveled, 98, *98*

for information transfer, 96

modulation of, 114, *114*

penetration of atmosphere, 45, *45*

transmission of, 48

rainbow, 47, *47*, 48, *48*

rarefaction, 11, *11*

ray diagram, 64, *64*

reasoning, 19, 37, 57, 77, 103, 121, 141

recorded audio, 100, *100*

recording studio design, *35*, 35–36

record player, 100

reflecting telescope, *87*, 89

reflection, 64

of color of light waves, 49, *49*, 55, 55–56, 67, 67–69

of light, 61, *61*, 62, 64, *64*, 77, 87, 89

of mechanical waves, 33, *33*, 39

with mirrors, 72–73

partial, 33

refraction, 66

of light, 66, 66–67, *67*, 73, 87, 89

optical illusions produced, *67*, *67*

relating to survival, 71

relationship

between amplitude and brightness, *51*, 51–54

between brightness and amplitude, *51*, *51*

between energy and amplitude, 15, *15*, 16, 21

of energy and frequency, 44

between frequency, wavelength, and amplitude, 48

between science and technology, 131, 135–138

between speed and frequency, 15

between wave period and frequency, 14–15

reliability, 118, 128

review

Lesson Self-Check, 19–21, 37–39, 57–59, 77–79, 86, 103–105, 121–123, 141–143, 150

Unit Review, 81–84, 145–148
Rjukan, Norway, 74, 74
ROY G BIV, 47

S

science
contribution to communication technology, 131, 131–134, 135
effect of digital signals on, 136, 136
relating to technology, 134
technology and, 131
use of computers, 138
scientific advancements, 134
seafloor map, 23, 23, 37, 37
secondary colors of light, 71, 71
Sessler, Gerhard, 17
sight
light requirement, 23, 61, 63, 67, 67–71, 77
needed for communication, 93, 93
signal, 93
advantage of digital signals, 126, 126
advantages of analog signals, 127, 127
analog and digital, 106–120, 108, **109,** 109, 110, 111, 113, 114, 115, 117, 118, 123, 136, 136
binary digital, 111, 111, 119, 119–120
effect of noise, 115–118
encoding and decoding, 94–95
identify types, 111
noise acquisition, 116, 116–120, 123, 123
storage noise, 118, 118
transformation of, 144
transmission noise, 118, 118
types of, 93, 93, 95, 105
smart phones, 132
Social Studies Connection
Radar in World War II, 80
When Radio Made Waves, 144
sound, volume of, 31
soundproofing, 35–36, 35
sound recordings, 100, 100

sound wave, 3, 3, **27,** 96
controlling to make music, 80
conversion of electric signal to, 144
dolphin communication with, 1
light waves compared to, 46, 46
limited range of, 96, 97
as mechanical waves, 24, 25, 25
medium for travel, 46
movement of energy, 24
sonogram and, 84
speed of in different media, 27, 27
spread of, 30–31, 30–31
transfer of energy, 24
transmission of, 32
visualization using, 23
space, 139–140
spacecraft, 91, 103, 103
special effects experts, 13, 16, 16
speed
of different wavelengths of light, 66
of electromagnetic waves, 98
of light, 44, 44, 67
of mechanical waves, 21
of radio waves, 98, 98
of sound waves through various media, 27, 27
of waves, 15
of waves at media boundaries, 34
steel, 28
frequency of sound in, 28
storage of information, 127, 127
sunlight
addition of noise to signals, 115
as source of electromagnetic waves, 45, 45
as source of light, 41, 41, 42, 48
as transverse waves, 41, 41
travel to Earth, 41, 41
wavelengths of light in, 48, 57, 57
supercomputer, 106, 106
surface of objects, 64
surface waves, 29, 29–30, 30
survival, 71

T

tables
binary code for letters, 120

of binary code for numbers, 112
of levels of brightness, 54
of LRV for paint colors, 56
of Morse code, 95
of observations, 10, 26
of properties of waves, 53
of speeds of waves in different media, 27
of temperatures, 138
of types of waves, 82
Why It Matters, 2, 88
Take It Further
AM and FM Radio Waves, 101–102
Careers in Engineering: Cell Tower Technician, 139–140
Designing Soundproof Rooms, 35–36
How Do Periscopes Work? 75–76
People in Science: James West, 17–18
Translating a Binary Signal, 119–120
What Color Should the Doghouse Be? 55–56
technology
for information transfer, 87, 87, 96, 142, 144
modes of communication, 89, 95, 97, 105, 105
radio, 97, 97, 142, 144
relating science to, 134
science and, 131
tectonic plates, 29
telegraph, 93, 93, 105, 132, 132
telephone, 95, 97, 97, 128, 129, 132, 132–133, 133, 143, 143, 145
telescope, 45, 68, 139
television, 97, 97
thermal energy, 31, 55
thermometer, 108, 108
3-level incandescent light bulb, 53–54
transfer of energy
from light to matter, 63
by waves, 6, 6–8, 7, 11, 11, 19, 19, 21, 21, 24, 24, 42, 42, 90
transfer of information
communication and waves, 144
communication technology, 124–140

through analog and digital signals, 106–120

translucent materials, 63, *63,* 67

transmission, 63

    of light, 63, *63, 66,* 67, 79

    of mechanical waves, 32, 39, *39*

    partial, 33

    of signals, 126, *126*

transparent material, *40,* **63,** *63,* 67, *67*

    of signals, 40

transverse wave, *42*

    crests and troughs of, 51, *51*

    in earthquakes, 12, *12*

    light as, 41, *41, 51,* 51–54

    as mechanical waves, 25, *25*

    motion of, 9, *9–12, 11,* 21, *21, 42*

    transfer of energy, 11, *11*

trough

    of light waves, 51

    of waves, 11, *11*

tsunami, 8, *8,* 24

U

ultrasound, *34*

ultraviolet wave, 43, *43,* 45, *45*

Unit Performance Task

    How can laser tag be improved? 149–150

    Will your audience be able to hear you? 85–86

Unit Project

    Design Wave Interactions, 3

    Emergency Broadcasting, 89

Unit Review, 81–84, 145–148

Unit Starter

    Modeling Light and Sound, 3

    Predicting the Path of Light, 89

V

vacuum, 41, 44, *44,* 66

variables in visible spectrum, 47, *47*

vibration with waves, 9, 24

vinyl record, 118, 127

visible light

    color of, 47, *47–48, 48*

as electromagnetic waves, 42

    penetration of atmosphere, 45, *45*

    refraction of, 66–69, *66, 67,* 68, *69*

vision, 42

volume of sound, 31

W

water

    frequency of sound in, 28, *28*

    speed of light through, *44*

water ripples, 11, 22, *22,* 29, *29–30, 30*

water wave, 1

    ocean waves, 4, *4,* 6, 24, *24*

    transfer of energy, 6, *6*

    tsunami compared to, 8, *8*

wave diagrams, 99, *99, 102*

wavelength, 13, *13,* 21

    color of light and, 47, *47–48, 48,* 59

    of electromagnetic waves, 43, 44

    encoding information into EM waves, 98, *98*

    energy related to, 44

    of light waves, 47

    media and, 28

    media boundaries and, 34

    relationship to amplitude and frequency, 48

    speed of light and, 66

    wave speed and, 15

wave period, *14,* 14–15, **15,** 21

waves

    amplitude and energy of, 15, *15,* 29

    amplitude and wavelength, 13

    analog and digital signals as, 110, *110,* 126

    blast waves, 13, *13,* 16

    combined type, 9, *9*–10, 11, 12, *12*

    communication and, 96

    of earthquakes, 9, *9*–10, 12, *12*

    longitudinal, 9, *9–12, 21*

    at media boundaries, 34

    modeling, 10–11

    modeling properties of, 52–54, *52*

    modulation of, 99–100

    in motion, *100*

    properties of, 21

    properties of at media boundaries, 34, *34*

    as pulse or repeating movement, 7, 21

    ripples on pond, 22, *22*

    speed of, 15, 21, 27, *27,* 34, 44, *44,* 98, *98*

    speed of at media boundaries, 34

    surface waves, *29, 29–30, 30*

    transfer of energy, 5–8, *6,* 7, 21, *21*

    transverse, 9, *9–12, 21,* 41, *41, 42*

    types of, 1

    unmodulated and modulated, 99, *99*–102, *100*

    wavelength, 34

    wave period, frequency, and speed, 14–15

    See also **electromagnetic (EM) waves; light; light wave; ocean wave; sound wave.**

wave speed, 15, 21, 27, *27*

West, James, 17–18

Whirlpool Galaxy, 125, *125,* 141, *141*

Why It Matters, 2, 88

X–Z

x-ray

    blocked by atmosphere, 45, *45*

    energy of, 44

    frequencies of, 43, *43*

    of teeth, 84, *84*

    transmission of, 68